The Way of the Crow

Antonio Arguello

Copyright © 2022 *Antonio Arguello*

All rights reserved

No part of this book may be reproduced, or stored in a retrieval system, or transmitted in any form or by any means, electronic, mechanical, photocopying, recording, or otherwise, without express written permission of the publisher. For information contact: Mariposa Book Transformation Services, 3120 Xenon Street, Wheat Ridge, CO 80215-6542. E-mail: aarguello@comcast.net

The characters and events portrayed in this
book are based on actual people and events.

Editor: Helena Mariposa

Associate Editor: William Coulter

Cover Design: Antonio Arguello All rights reserved
               Timothy Arguello

Photography: Antonio Arguello All rights reserved

Illustrations: Antonio Arguello All rights reserved

Published by Mariposa Book Transformation Services
             helenamariposa@comcast.net
             aarguello@comcast.net

ISBN 978-0-578-28224-4 (pbk.)

For my wife
Helena Mariposa

> As long as there is hope
> There is no hope.
> When there is no hope
> Then there is hope.
> Hope is the great deceiver.
> —Antonio Arguello

Contents

Introduction	1
Chapter 1. Return of the Cat	7
Chapter 2. Priest as Magician	15
Chapter 3. Turtle	24
Chapter 4. White Buffalo Woman	31
Chapter 5. Spider and the Baby	37
Chapter 6. The Dark Side	43
Chapter 7. Shaman's World View	48
Chapter 8. Decent: Shamanic Journey	51
Chapter 9. Treasure Map	54
Chapter 10. The Great Master of Ecstasy	57
Chapter 11. In Search of Merlin's Sword	61
Chapter 12. The Myth of Death	69
Chapter 13. Anima	72
Chapter 14. Sublimatio	76
Chapter 15. Calcinatio	82
Chapter 16. Solutio	92
Chapter 17. Buried Alive	94
Chapter 18. Time and Space	119
Chapter 19. 2060	125
Chapter 20. Lions, Tigers and Bears	135
Chapter 21. Spirituality vs. Religion	146
Chapter 22. The Gaia Hypothesis	148
Chapter 23. Call Me Kikta	153
Chapter 24. Return of Merlin	157
Chapter 25. Self-Destruction	160
Chapter 26. Covid-19	163
Chapter 27. The Technical Shaman	167
Chapter 28. Burn This One	171
Chapter 29. Healing Journey	178
Chapter 30. The Reluctant Shaman	181
Chapter 31. AK-47	184
Chapter 32. Return Home	187
Bibliography	191
About Antonio	192

Crow taught me to look out one eye and see this world, then to look out the other eye and see the other world. I have lived my life perceiving in this way—through one eye to see the world as it is and the other eye to see the other realm. And in writing this book, I did the same.

Introduction

In the tradition of the adventurer, the following is a journey through a labyrinth into the world of a Twenty-First Century Shaman. It is not meant as an intellectual discourse on the magico-religious phenomenon, but rather a rambling overview of experiences and observations made during my many years of practice and study. It is a sojourn along an unknown and unmarked excursion into the lower realm of the psyche. It is at times terrible and savage, and at other times sublime and elevated to divine heights.

Just the other side of the dream is the infinite world of the "Shaman's Journey," where dragons, demons, wizards, and gods wait for those willing and brave enough to venture there. It is a dimension where the relativity of ordinary consciousness is suspended, where time and space become clay to be molded by the hands of the wizard.

The role of the Shaman is to enter that timeless space, create maps of the terrain, learn the cosmology, acquire wisdom, and return to share and to become the guide. But it is not without cost. The price is dismemberment, death, and having to face the demons that reside there and feed on the human energies of despair, fear, anger, and their seething ilk. Like the Sumerian account of Inanna, queen of the heavens, who descends through seven gates into the lower world, stripped of all her possessions and finally her very flesh and then hung on a hook, so the journeyer must descend first into the lower world, face the demons, be devoured by the beast, and emerge transformed. It is also about glimpses of the infinite, the heights, and the presence of the divine within us.

What differentiates the Twenty-First Century Shaman from his predecessors is the access to information. Whereas previously Shamans had access only to their lineage or mentors, the Twenty-First Century Shamans have access to a whole body of works related to the practice. In addition, we have entered a time of accelerated change and innovation to the point that the vast store of knowledge is boundless. Our lives are literally enmeshed in this web of ones and zeros. The amount of data zipping around the world is phenomenal. One can pinpoint any place on earth with a few clicks on an electronic device. Phones used by children have more computing power than a room full of computers from our recent past. This accelerated and exponential technological advancement has led many to declare the end of the Anthropocene era and the epoch of the Novacene era, the age of hyperintelligence.

We exist in a world of twenty-first century issues of disconnection and at the same time constant connection. The Shaman must have an ever-expanding view and grasp of the evolving culture and recognize all related influences and the impact this has on the individual and the world. The idea that we are a wired world is never truer. Whereas our early predecessors dealt with the village issues and concerns, our present issues and concerns are of the global village. The global shadow is at our doorstep, and the hollow knock at the door by our future resonates loud and clear. The immediate future looks bleak, but there is a collective awareness and movement by activists creating solutions.

I call on Healers, Medicine people, Light Workers, Shamans, Religious leaders, and all others engaged in serving humanity to recruit and involve others in the movement to salvage our future. Humanity stands on the brink of a chasm, and behind us is our future inching us closer and closer to the brink.

With the collective energy working toward a sustainable future, children will be able to walk into a brighter, more evolved world. Every single person is affected by the chaos unfolding around us, and it will require the concerted involvement of all to redirect the destructive path we are on. And on the brighter side, movements are being initiated around the world by diverse groups recognizing the needs of our future as a diversely inhabited planet. It is important to remember that even the smallest of actions has an impact.

When first I ventured into this abyss of climate change and social injustice, the trail remained hidden, overgrown with optimism, vagaries, ignorance, and misinformation meant to keep us blind and stumbling in the darkness. As I stumbled along the rocky path, I uncovered truths and information I did not want to know, but there they were, blinding truths. But they also revealed the twists, the turns, the drops in the trail trod by the few. Among them is Sir David Attenborough who in a 60 Minutes interview stated "a crime has been committed against the planet."

At the same time, we can look to our immediate past for answers, to the angst we perceived during this era of turmoil and confusion. The answers are there for the seekers who dare to tread on the path of self-discovery. Trails have been blazed, breadcrumbs dropped, but one must know how to look and how to distinguish these signs. This is where Joseph Campbell, C.G. Jung, and so many others enter the equation. This is not a treatise on these dedicated scholars. There is already a multitude of books and information on and by these wizards. The goal here is to elucidate some basic information. What is a Shaman, particularly the Twenty-First Century Shaman? What are their roles and responsibilities? What are the issues that are facing our global community? And finally, to encourage the community to engage these issues by whatever means are available to them.

Quantum field theorists and Shamans delve into the mysteries of creation and destruction at the most basic levels where energy is the force to be mastered. Like the theorist the Shaman seeks to destroy and recreate the energy forces found there, particle by particle, and then observe it recreate itself from the stripped bleached bones of its former self. The hope is for a greater understanding of a global community and our impact on the environment and consequently the future of humanity.

Most Shamans I have encountered are also artists with the most creative expressions imaginable. My belief is that most original art comes from somewhere deep within the psyche, and because Shamans wander there so often, they encounter images rich and often mythical. The images seen throughout this text are larger than life-size sculptures drawn from those depths.

The images were born as paintings on a wall done by an artist friend and Jungian psychologist, Claudine Jeanrenaud, PhD. The paintings were fantastical and two dimensional. The piece above that I call the "Grandfather," as it was the first of the generation, is three dimensional but still limited. The following sculptures became increasingly three dimensional until they freed themselves entirely from the walls. The figure I refer to as the "Giant" stands alone and is the largest and most imposing of the group. A final figure is planned that will be animated, propelled by an operator, will emit laser light from its eyes and spit fire from its mouth, and will stalk the earth standing ten feet tall.

Each figure is infused with energy that it is felt by viewers. I ask them to tell me a story of any one figure that speaks to them, and they inform me what energy each piece contains or expresses to them. The one reaction I felt was most telling came from a Lakota native woman. She said, "These are spirits wearing clothes."

I offer here a view into the workings and meanderings of one brooding Shaman, the hopes, dreams, observations, and visions. This is my alembic. An alchemical container in which many elements are introduced in the quest for the gold, the sought-after elemental truth.

Grandfather: From the Cave Gallery sculpture collection.
They are beginning to take on a life of their own.

Chapter 1

Return of the Cat

My story begins many years ago and involves a series of three visions separated by decades and calls up a succession of timeless images. It is the retelling of a shamanic initiation of death and rebirth. It began with a ten- or eleven-year-old boy in dreamtime, the time of no boundaries and of endless possibilities, from the dimension where jade encrusted dragons and tassel fringed-flying carpets swooped through lapis skies.

I can tell this story as I was that boy living with my parents in our humble home, a rambling adobe structure-built block by brown-mud block by my father's hand from the very ground on which it stood. I remember it as a home where tortillas shaped by my sisters, hot from the comal, were spread with butter that dripped down my chin in warm rivulets. I wanted for naught. I knew no fear. That is, until that night, in dreamtime, the Great Black Cat prowled into my life.

Vision

I had wandered into the kitchen, a simple room with a wood burning stove, and with chucks of jet-black coal in a gray tin bucket and a pile of newly chopped wood with which to cook the supper meal. I sat at the worn-pine table I had known all my life and watched my mother stir the potatoes frying in a blackened cast iron skillet and my sisters setting the table. The tantalizing smell of roasting green chili peppers in the oven promised yet another meager but tasty meal.

I was the first to see the Great Cat, a black shadow circling the house, sniffing at the doors, and chuffing at the windows. It stood larger than any ordinary great cat. Its muscled body gleamed in its surefooted stride as it paced restlessly before the window. It watched me as it would a plump prairie dog, and I knew that it was there to consume me. And I was consumed, but by uninitiated fear. As the Cat appraised me with its bright yellow knowing eyes, I trembled with heart pounding terror.

Naturally, the family panicked. My father, decisive as always, quickly boarded up the windows and open doors with an ironing board, doors from cupboards, and wooden planks. There remained one doorway that led to another room that had a door that did not fit properly. My father, never believing in waste of any kind, used everything, and had used this door even though it had left a two or three-inch gap at the top.

The dark beast had managed its way into the house and consumed one of the family before we had a chance to escape safely into the kitchen. The rest of us gathered there in terror, clinging to one another, and praying loudly to the Virgin Mary for deliverance from this evil.

It prowled around inside the house, and we

could hear its loud grunts and snarls. Finally, Cat found its way to the door with the gap. It peered in at me. Its gleaming eye measured me in anticipation. I shrank away in deathly fear. My heart felt like it would burst, and I prayed to be free from the dark threat.

Somehow, through the grayness of near death I concocted a plan. What I realized was that this dark manifestation was most powerful and could easily rip through this door. I reasoned that it either did not want to or did not know that it could. But I knew that it could, that it possessed a power beyond the ordinary. I decided that when it again looked in through that gap, I would stick a knife into that searching eye. I went to the knife drawer and chose an old, long, carbon-steel bladed knife, its surface gray, its edge dull. Cat again appeared at the gap and stared unblinking at me. I shuddered but quickly approached and plunged the blade into that fearsome yellow eye. The blade stabbed roughly into the Cat's brain. The Cat dropped away with an ear-searing howl. I awoke in fear-tinged sweat and trembling, yet relieved to be free of that dark beast.

Time passed. The apparition forgotten, lost in the passages of time and age. In the interval I had become an adult, studied, and practiced the ancient arts of meditation and Eastern disciplines.

Until one warm summer night, sometime between then and now, a second vision occurred again in dreamtime, desecrating the temple of sleep. I was living in my own home, an adult lying in the comfort and safety of my suburban bedroom. A full moon shone, and the neat yards of suburbia slumbered in dark shadow and pearly light. The sounds of the night brushed lightly against my reverie, crickets, a dog barking in the distance, a fan hummed softly at the window.

Slowly, I sensed a difference in the night that I could not account for. It had become quiet, too still, as though time had become thick and heavy. A sound, more intrusive than usual night sounds, pricked at my senses. It disturbed me. I attempted to ignore it. I told myself it would pass if I gave it no attention, lent it no energy. Yet it persisted and reached deep into my unconscious, into the black depths of hidden fears. I knew what it was, yet still fought to contain it in the cold graveyard of old bones and rusted iron fences that was my shadow. It would not be contained. In renewed form, Cat reappeared from its subterranean lair.

Cat had returned, larger, more menacing and had manifested there to consume me. I now laid quieted by terror in my deathbed where I had just moments before lain in ignorant safety. The door to my room stood open and inviting to any intrusion from the shadowed night, which now hummed with charged energy. My body quivered, my mind challenged the reality of what was happening, and my heart struggled against my ribs in truth-knowing terror. Cat was in the house, coming down the hall. Its claws clicked softly against the dulled oak flooring that would now never see refinishing. I had no means of escape or defense.

Guttural warnings punctuated the panting

and patient breath of this harbinger of nocturnal death. I, on the other hand, dared not breathe lest it give away my presence. Then the darkness filled the doorway. My pounding heart revealed my cowering person to my yellow-eyed tormentor. My fate stood yards away. I lay paralyzed in fear and drenched sweat. Cat crossed the threshold and in one leap, a fluid arch, stood majestically poised at my bedside.

Yet in that fated trembling moment I reassured myself, *Ah. There is a means of escape here. Remember your training. This is but a vision.* In desperation, as Cat gathered itself above me, I struggled to free myself from this vision. And just as Cat reached for my throat with its open jaws of stained ivory-colored fangs, dripping with anticipation, I reached into my vision and wrenched my soul free of the inevitable death-dealing strike. Cat vanished back into the murky depths to lay dormant, waiting for an unguarded moment when it could finish its task of dismemberment of my soul. Once again, I had thwarted the beast, first by fight, now by flight.

Time in its inevitable way passed and Cat was relegated to the dustbin of memory. Then a decade or so later, a third and final vision occurred. I sat in meditation before my simple alter, the sweet smell of burning sage heavy on the air, peaceful in joyful repose, reflecting on the fortunes of my life, and the resolved sorrows and regrets of the past.

Gradually, I found myself outdoors in a lush meadow, the sky clear, the air fresh, pine trees to the front and to the left and right of the clearing. Behind me scrub oak bushes rustled in the breeze. The smell of forest compost lingered on the air. I breathed deeply taking the earthy smells deep into my lungs when my ear caught a sound in the bushes. I held my breath. I strained to hear, not wanting to accept what prowled in the bushes, pacing, watching. Cat had returned. My heart seized in my chest and the knowing exploded in my entire body. My every cell quivered, every atom responded and shrank in terror. Cat had returned.

I looked to the left and there in the distant trees rustled by a breeze, entities began arriving. There stood a counsel of five glowing figures that had a human shape but no distinct features. Their light pulsed faintly blue to green. They conferred among themselves in hushed and urgent tones. I could not hear their discussion.

From behind me the dark menace brushed aside the foliage in a passing whisper. Its massive paws a soft leaf-treading footfall in contrast to the heavy thud of my heart against my ribs. I will sit here very still, I decided. Maybe Cat won't see me, maybe Cat won't think I am food if I don't run. Also, I knew I was being watched by the figures in the trees beyond the meadow. Cat approached me from behind until it stood at my back. I trembled and labored to breath. A thick musky animal odor hung heavy about me. The rumbling throaty sounds vibrated the very air I sucked into my lungs. Heat from its body enveloped me. The panting moist breath of Cat on my neck made my hair stand on end. It bristled. Cat circled me, once brushing against me, its fur rough, scratchy. Then it sat a bit to my right. I squeezed my eyes tight, hoping to shut out this horror.

I knew right then, *Okay, I'm going to die. There is no escape this time. I cannot fight, I cannot run.* "But," I pleaded, "give me a quick, merciful death, please. I will not struggle. I do not want to be mangled and torn to bits."

Trembling, I offered my throat to Cat knowing their preferred way of killing is through suffocation. Cat approached, and I prepared to feel the Cat's fangs sink into my throat. Instead, a cough, then a great dry, rough tongue licked the right side of my face, its breath hot and humid. It scratched my face from bottom to top opening my right eye in the process. And there before me hung this massive dark head. Cat then withdrew, and I was confused. Cat circled me once again in the opposite direction and sat directly opposite me.

At that point, I transformed into a great cat. I had become a black panther also but of normal great cat size. I looked to my left at the entities. One of them nodded to the others and they took leave. I said to myself, *Yes*. I understood I had passed a test. In that same moment, had several insights. I understood that I had acquired one of the most important lessons I needed to learn, the "art of transformation." In that act of accepting death, I acquired my power ally, Cat, and my great fear of death had been transformed into power, personal power, of equal strength to that of the Cat. My first vision at ten years old occurred after the death of an aunt, my first encounter with death that manifested as Cat.

The other knowing was that I was to begin working with others to help guide them in their spiritual quest in the same way I had worked on myself and that I was to become a Shaman. I had been summoned. This was that traditional shamanic initiation.

I now wield a magic sword. It is certainly double edged and powerful. The dragon entered my life on a wisp of consciousness just prior to the appearance of a mythical sword. I am a Shaman, like Hermes, a guide of souls and have arrived here from a constricted ego-oriented existence. One in which I worked a job day after day, year after year, much as my father did in the mines. I toiled as a "gatekeeper" at a warehouse for wounded souls who were rabid by the time they walked through the doors of the Maximum-Security unit for the criminally insane. Too stressed to have much vision of any other life, I provided for my family. Like my father before me, I was a provider. Now, my consciousness expanded through education, spiritual practices, work, and life experiences, I have entered the realm of King Arthur and the Grail, and yes, scaly fire-breathing dragons. I have seen the underbelly of what and who we are and have journeyed to the outer reaches of mythical and spiritual realms.

Now, decades later I am old and tired, but it does not matter as I have experienced the great mystery, life, with everything that goes along with it, and I now have my ally, a great Black Cat who walks by my side to protect me and support me when I stumble.

Chapter 2

The Priest as Magician

I am a Twenty-First Century Shaman. Without intention or desire, life's circumstances shaped my course as does a river making its way to the open sea. Prior to this, all I had known was the safety of my family and the teachings of love by the nuns at the catholic school I attended. These "Sisters Mary, pointer in hand" teachers took their task of shaping catholic minds quite seriously. Their black habits spoke of supreme authority, and they never failed to command my attention. When they posed the question, "What is God?" I responded with the prescribed answer, "God is Love."

My immersion in spirituality came at an early age. Under the tutelage of nuns and priests my soul soared with angels and plummeted to the burning fires of hell. The concept of the battle between good and evil took on form and meaning. Spirits dwelt undisturbed in my house.

The ritual of High Mass introduced the priestly magician, one who could transform wine into blood and bread into the body of Christ. But even as I accepted the Host I broke one of the ten commandments, thou shalt not covet, for I secretly wanted the role of the altar boy who stood alongside the priest and chanted the Latin responses, rang the chimes, and smudged the congregation with incense. The rituals never failed to transport me to ecstatic realms where I could commune directly with the Divine. It was a time and place where pleas uttered in reverent supplication soared beyond the high vaulted ceilings of the brown stone church.

It was quite comforting to be in the hands of those who would teach me all I needed to know to exist in my world. I knew that the nuns understood the mysteries of life, the universe, and everything. They provided me with ritual milestones to mark my passage through the temporal form and onto greater glory—heaven.

From Baptism to ashes, I knew what was going to happen and what to expect when I got there. I also knew that if I had forbidden thoughts, I could spend eternity with the dark prince of Perdition. It was understood that impure thoughts and evil forces existed in the world but that one should not dwell on these lest they take command of one's eternal soul, and it be damned for eternity. The shadow began to take on form. Impulses and selfish desires were banished to the basement of the house where they lay dormant, waiting for the doors to be opened by the hero on a quest for the treasure hidden beyond the darkness in some musty forgotten cave. But that would have to await the one with the keys and the courage to enter and face the fire of the dragon's breath.

Those early times with the nuns and priests were the roots of my calling that would involve many levels of consciousness. From the basement of the house to the eves of the church I have continued to explore with a dedication I have not always understood. My fascination with consciousness has led me to places not everyone would want to go. But I have learned to face the stark truth of what it means to be human, in all its glory and in all its shame.

One cannot speak of consciousness without stirring the cauldron of spirituality. It can be said that spirituality is the manifestation of the functions of consciousness and that consciousness is the source of God, a nameless, faceless totality, the whole of creation. Whereas I use the term Spirit to refer to that which is our living essence.

What, exactly, is consciousness? I do not know. This is what I do know. It cannot be defined or explained. It is the unknowable. But it can be experienced and those experiences understood. One can only speak of its "nature," as one would of a dark, mysterious, and magical woman who happens upon one's path, lingers, and then is gone. To some she would be a dark Madonna, a mother, a goddess, and to others a whore, a temptress, a lover. Each would know her in the context of their own experiences and would understand something of her nature. And so, it is similar in that one understands consciousness in terms of one's experiences with its nature.

Reality occurs within the matrix of consciousness. It is perceived primarily through the senses, filtered through the oceanic field of consciousness, and played back to the world as a response, a perception. The shape or the color of that reality is dependent on the memories and experiences which exist within the field as psychic energy.

Consensual reality, the existence of the material world is the gross expression of reality, and beyond the ordinary perception lies the infinite realm of consciousness. The material aspect is not separate and is part and parcel to a greater whole of infinite reality.

The nature of reality for the Shaman is decidedly different from that of the non-Shaman in that the Shaman rearranges the field to recreate reality as he chooses at any given moment.

Shamans and scientists are not at odds in their worldviews. Science has observed the basic structures or essence of the material body and at its core found energy. Scientists put their glassy eye to the electron microscope and observe the atom. The Shaman puts his ancient and torn ear to its bony chest and proclaims, "It lives, it is alive!" and names this basic essence, Spirit. It is the same energy, given life. Shamans study and call on it to affect other energies or spiritual forces that abound in his world.

Conceptual time or linear progression as it occurs in history books is also a feature of the material plane. From a squinty-eyed shamanic view, linear time is another facet of a larger luminous jewel. The shamanic practitioner wraps himself in an elaborately adorned blanket of time woven of multiple understandings and perceptions to tread upon the long-forgotten paths of the ancestors and on paths yet unmarked. Linear time is useful in a world where B follows A, and C follows B, but in the world of nonmatter where time and space have no relevancy, where yesterday, today, and tomorrow coexist as one.

Just the other side of the dream is the infinite world of the shaman's journey, where dragons, demons, wizards, and gods wait for those willing and brave enough to venture there. It is a dimension where the relativity of ordinary consciousness is suspended, where time and space become clay to be molded by the hands of the wizard.

The shamanic journey is an altered state of consciousness induced by the Shaman for the purpose of accessing the spirit realm and normally unconscious material. The goal of the shamanic journey is to expand consciousness. And in the process to guide journeyers through their unresolved conflicts to integrated wholeness. Transformation of psychic energy is at the core of the healing process.

The Lessons of the Shaman

The lessons of the Shaman are contained in our collective history and in the myths by which we live, consciously or unconsciously. To live consciously, fully consciously, is the goal of the Shaman. By means of the shamanic journey, one enters the realms of consciousness that reside beyond our ordinary senses. It is a place from where magic emanates and where dark regions exist that direct all that we do, think, and become, unconsciously living out the myths by which we fulfill our roles. Fully conscious implies that one is familiar and connected to that which resides below and beyond ordinary consciousness, beyond the personal, and to the collective unconscious. Upon entering an altered state of consciousness, doors begin opening and vistas are laid out for exploration.

In each religion of every culture there are practices whose sole purpose is to achieve the altered state. Be it prayer, meditation, chant, peyote, or whirling dervish, the methodology connects one to the spiritual, moves one into the realm of the mythical to commune with higher consciousness. Shamanic practice is thousands of years old, a tested and proven methodology for dealing with the issues we as humans share. For centuries the drum has been one of the Shaman's vehicles of transport and whose voice has reached through time to connect us to the primal heartbeat. The drum is the horse that carries one into and through the lower world.

History reveals that as we engage the twenty-first century, messages of doom will flourish. But unlike former times, these present-day utterances will ring loud and true. The space we call Earth is finite in terms of resources or the ability to safely absorb the toxic lifestyles of man. As Earth's population explodes, every problem will be magnified ten times. Humans have the capacity to affect every ecosystem on Earth and have provided poor stewardship at every level. There is no reason to believe that that practice will be altered. The Shaman lives in the past, the present, and the future, and in doing so, can heal the past and foresee the future. Never has there been a greater need for Shamans than the twenty-first century. Had mankind's consciousness advanced at the same rate as our technology, the Earth would instead be a paradise.

The Shaman has a vast understanding and knowledge of consciousness or, in shamanic terms, the spirit world. Were I to travel to any country and seek out a Shaman by whatever name he or she is called, they would recognize me as a practitioner and our terminology and methodology would be compatible. The drum, the rattle, the altered state, and the methodologies are all universal. The worldview of an upper, middle, and lower world is also consistent with contemporary views of consciousness, namely conscious, subconscious, and unconscious.

Alchemy

The work of C. G. Jung, based on alchemical, archetypal, and mythical observation, will be demonstrated throughout this text, but it is not meant to be a comprehensive presentation.

C.G. Jung chose to use the operations of alchemy as a metaphor for the psychic processes of individuals undergoing psychotherapy. He believed that transformation, change, and growth in an individual could be expressed using alchemical symbolism. There are twelve such processes but only a few will be mentioned in this presentation. They are *Prima Materia, Solutio, Calcinatio, Coagulatio, Coniunctio,* and *Sublimatio.* These processes can be presented from a wide range of perspectives, all of which can be recognized by their central theme.

Alchemy is thought to be a lost and ancient practice, but it is in fact a reference to much-misunderstood symbolic processes of transformative stages of ego development. It is imperative to note that the examples presented herein are the gross illustrations of these operations as they pertain to the shamanic experience. The application in relation to psychotherapy is not discussed.

Alchemical process begins with *Prima Materia*. This refers to a substance in its unrefined state, an undifferentiated condition, or innocence as a child. It has potential for a higher purpose if it has been subjected to or has undergone an alchemical process. We begin as *Prima Materia*, basic undifferentiated ego. As one progresses through life, the ego is subjected to influences which shape the individual. The final goal is gold, the illuminated Self. These processes are often reported in dreamwork, psychotherapy, and shamanic journey work. Their relationship to psychotherapy is elucidated in literature by C.G. Jung, Edward F. Edinger, Joseph Campbell, and others who have demonstrated considerable insight into the development of the psyche and ego constructs.

Solutio is associated with water or any liquid. Its central theme involves the act of cleansing, dissolving, or disappearing, in which some form of transformation occurs.

Calcinatio is related to fire, and anything having to do with fire is the process where something can be burned, cleansed, melted, or destroyed resulting in transformation. It can be related to burning passions or intense feelings. In all these operations one must recognize the feelings, the psychic process being played out. Is it a heated scenario?

Coagulatio is related to an earth element. It involves concretization or solidification of that which previously was in an undifferentiated state, which would result in transformation to a new or different compound. In other words, *Coagulatio* is usually the result of actions that cause concretization of dreams, inner processes, values, and insights, and thus is involved in the process of Individuation. *Coagulatio* can also be seen as that process of solidifying one's psyche as opposed to a fragmented ego. Once again, we can see that the development and transformation of the ego can be stated in alchemical terms. This state of *Coagulatio* is generally the result of the other alchemical operations, such as

Solutio and/or *Calcinatio*. The alchemical processes are not concrete in nature when used in an analytical context. They are more like a stream passing before you. It is the same stream but with different faces.

Sublimatio is the operation pertaining to air and derives from the Latin *sublimis* meaning "high" and refers to an elevating process whereby a low substance is translated into a higher form by an ascending movement. It turns the material into air by volatilizing and elevating it, much like a solid when heated, passes directly into a gaseous state. Mountains, stairs, flying, or climbing often indicate this process. An altered psychic state in which the body is transformed to a spiritual body is an example of *Sublimatio*.

When dealing with development and transformation of an individual, it is helpful to encapsulate psychic processes in alchemical symbolism and metaphor. It is important for the Shaman to envision these processes in the broadest context, including the feelings and emotions generated during the developmental progression. These alchemical themes are prevalent in psychotherapy, dreamwork, depth psychology, and Shaman's journey work. Due to their organic nature, they are universal and apply to humankind across the ages.

THE WAY OF THE CROW

The Big Guy: From the Cave Gallery Sculpture Collection.
They are finally free from the wall!

Chapter 3

Turtle

What better way to introduce one to the realms of the Shaman and demonstrate the alchemical processes involved than by immersion into the unknown of an individual's psyche. The unknown, where few have gone and those that have done so have emerged changed in profound ways, their absolute certainty of what they knew and who they were was shattered and replaced with a greater Self.

By way of introduction, I give you Anna, a woman of middle age with two children. She ventured into the world of the Shaman out of a desire to resolve crippling emotional issues. She had been resisting journeying for a couple of months because the thought of it scared her. On January 15, 1992, she told me she finally ran out of excuses and had built up the courage to journey. She explained to me that her resistance and anxiety had come from her childhood and her upbringing.

"I was reared in a small Colorado town. My father was a roofer and mother did not work out of the home until I was in junior high school. Every Sunday, we attended Sunday school and then church services afterwards. I was raised a Baptist in a small, conservative, blue collar town. I was baptized, married, and taught Sunday school in the same church. My two children were dedicated in it. My parents still attend this church, and both my sisters remain Baptists, attending nearby churches.

"I knew Satan existed, as did his demons. I had been taught that one stayed away from things that might be his dominion, drinking, dancing, the supernatural, etc. Your talk of journeying to the lower world brought to my mind Satan and Hell. Now if that wasn't going into Satan's realm, I don't know what would be.

"I really don't understand what you are talking about, and I'm afraid."

I encouraged her to ask questions, to clarify things for herself. So, she asked questions, lots of questions. As she questioned me, she said, "Now I am curious to try journeying. I still believe I will meet some demons, but after talking with you, I understand they will be my demons. They will be my issues to confront and deal with, not Satan trying to claim my soul." Even though still afraid, she told me she needed to try it and agreed to try at least one journey.

Prior to entering the Journey room, I instructed her on how to proceed and what to expect. I shared with her that there are three levels in the Spirit realm of the journey: the upper world, the middle world (the one we lived in), and the lower world. For the first journey, she was to go to the lower world. I advised her to envision a place where she could enter the lower world, one that was familiar to her, her safe place, such as an old tree with deep roots, a pool, the ocean, any opening that would serve as a portal, a gateway.

I gave her the intent of the first journey and a destination.

The intent was to experience the journey and find any allies that might present themselves, and the destination was a place of safety that would be familiar to her. One in which she would feel comfortable.

I explained that while journeying one must seek out and engage at least four essential allies: 1. An ally for courage. 2. An ally for protection, should one feel threatened. 3. An ally for strength, physical strength, to combat foes. 4. An ally to serve as a guide, to prevent wandering aimlessly in the void. The number and type of ally entities is endless, from magicians to teachers to whatever the Journeyer requires to accomplish their goal and will be addressed in greater detail later. I made it clear that she would not necessarily meet all or any of her allies during her first journey, but she should be on the lookout for them.

Finally, I explained to Anna how there is life in all things, even the stones, and that the room we were about to go into was a space made sacred with ritual. I told her to remove all trappings of this world: jewelry, watches, and our shoes. We entered with only the clothes on our backs. I burned sage and used the smoke to purify Anna and myself. We sat on cushions with candles burning all around the room. I gave her more instructions on how to proceed to the underworld and what to expect.

I had her do some deep breathing exercises and meditate briefly. Later she reported that during the meditation, she saw the chalk cliffs close to her parents' cabin and explained that they have always been special to her. She went on to tell me that the cliffs are pocked with caves, and she saw a large cave and knew where she would go to begin her journey.

After meditating she laid down, and I covered her with blankets and made her comfortable. I explained that she would be taking a spiritual journey and would not need her physical body. She would need to leave her physical self comfortably on sacred ground. I began by using relaxation techniques to prepare her for the journey.

The following is a self-reported account.

Anna's First Journey

So, I began. I began a shamanic journey.

The drumming began. It surrounded me, becoming one with me. My heartbeat slowed to the rhythm of the drum. I drifted, my body laid heavy on the floor and my spirit rose to the cave I had chosen. I stood just outside the cave for quite some time, still frightened, but knowing I needed to go in there. I entered cautiously. It was very dark. The outside of the cave seemed illuminated. Then rays of light spread across the top of the cavern, moving across in ripples. I moved to just inside the cave's entrance. I saw a spiral tunnel. It was moving. I looked down, and there was a light at the end. I knew I had to get to the light. I floated down towards the light, then the tunnel faded. I stood in the cavern again while rays of light moved across the ceiling. I tried the spiral three or four times but to my dismay, I couldn't get to the bottom.

Frustrated, I left the tunnel and wandered through the cave. During this time, light, fluffy clouds moved rapidly across the cavern. The rippling light played through them. I came to an arch made of white crystals. The crystals gave off the only substantial light in the cavern. I looked at the arch from all angles, up one side, across the top and down the other side. I looked at it closely. I had never seen anything so beautiful. The crystals glittered and gave off plenty of light for me to see. I passed the arch and saw the image of a hawk or an eagle. I saw only a half-formed image of its head. It quickly disappeared.

I moved to the left. Fluttering just beside a lighted outcropping at a bend in the cave, a light shone. The light was not round. It was long and rather vaporous. It reminded me of a fairy, and I knew the entity was female. Curious about this fairy-like being, my frustration vanished. She told me telepathically that I had to turn that corner, it was the way. I did as she said. I immediately came to a rushing waterfall. Rainbows formed above the shimmering pond below.

I stood at the top, studying the waterfall, aware there had to be an opening behind the water. I wanted to get down to the pool below and to the opening I knew was there. I wondered how to descend and considered the water for some time. Suddenly I felt confident and took a step forward. I glided down to the bottom of the falls. Looking for the opening, I walked under the water. I looked up and the water washed over me. I felt cleansed. The sun shone through the water.

I remained there quite some time, marveling at the beauty. Then I turned to follow the stream. I had found no opening behind the falls. An image began to form or was moving closer. I made out the shape of a turtle.

I said, "Hi, Turtle, thank you for coming.

Are you going to show me the way?" Turtle motioned for me to follow. I knew we were connected. We began to move downstream with Turtle leading the way.

About this time, the Shaman called me back. I could hear him calling my name. I went quickly back to my cave and exited. I had been gone thirty-five minutes, but it felt like I had only been gone ten minutes.

The first journey is about gaining experience and developing trust in one's abilities and judgement to deal with whatever presents itself. On review of the journey, I assured her that she had indeed successfully experienced a shamanic journey, which brought her much delight. She expressed surprise that she had not only gone to the lower world but had actually been able to interact within that realm.

First, we processed the cleansing beneath the falls. She realized she felt a release of fear, anxiety, and doubt. I pointed out that she had interacted with potential allies, the turtle as a guide, and the vaporous female entity whose role had not been identified yet, letting her know that they may return in future Journey sessions. We also touched briefly on alchemy and the function of water in the transformative process. It became clear to her that the experience was more complex than she had initially understood. After our follow up, she grasped the significance of the events in the journey with understanding, acceptance, and greater self-assurance.

When she left the sacred space, her shoulders were no

longer curved downward in a protective pose, her hands weren't fidgeting, and she no longer avoided eye contact. Instead, she stood tall in a relaxed posture, looked straight at me when we spoke, and smiled as she thanked me.

Chapter 4

White Buffalo Woman

Anna returned the following week ready to jump right into a journey. I informed her we needed to discuss what she had experienced and how to proceed before beginning. She shared the contrast she had observed between how she felt now and how she had felt before her first journey. She marveled at the amount of resistance she had felt prior to her first journey in contrast to how eager she felt on this day. "I realized while discussing my experience with a friend," Anna said, "that I have begun an incredible adventure, one that could change my life forever."

I started by explaining to Anna that just as there are demons, there are also allies that manifest as personal strengths. Therefore, one of her tasks would be to dialogue with the allies she had met and would meet to establish a relationship with them. For instance, if frightened or threatened, she needed to call on an ally for courage, or if lost, she needed to call on an ally that is a guide to direct her. Yet again the intent of this journey is to find her other allies and to see where they and the journey takes her.

We entered the journey room, I smudged the space and Anna, and began drumming. As I said before, the drum is considered to be the horse that carries one into and through the journey. It is an integral part of the Shaman's medicine bundle.

And so, we began.

Anna's Second Journey

I began at the mouth of the cave and called for the female entity from my last journey while I stood at the opening, and she was there before I even went in, just inside the entrance. The entity was at first the same size as before. She grew and filled my range of vision with light, glowing shimmering light, sort of pink in color with golds and pure white. She was stunning, and I told her she was. She said, "Thank you."

We started to move as she shrank and moved down a slope. I asked, while she was in the large light stage, "Are you my guide?"

She said, "Yes. I am to guide you through all."

As we moved down the slope, I asked "What is your name?"

She said, "Cassandra."

We turned a corner to the right and were in a Mexican village. It was a small village; the houses were adobe and square with flat roofs. The adobe had a pinkish hue. There were people who went about their business. The feeling was of activity, but friendliness. They smiled as they went their way. The sun shone bright. It was a warm and beautiful day. We left there and began to climb a rocky slope when I remembered the arch.

"Cassandra," I said, "I need to see the arch again."

She took me to another huge cavern that was

within mine. Crystals covered the walls and ceiling, but these were different. They were not illuminated. We walked on. Cassandra floated, and we came to my arch. I stepped very close to get a good look and then melted into it, became part of it very briefly, and then came out on the other side.

I saw an old, but well-kept small frame house, gray with white trim. It sat desolate in the mountains on a field. There was a slope behind it and plenty of trees.

I then came back through. I asked Cassandra if I could have a crystal. She said yes, took one off, and handed it to me. It continued to glow in my hand. It was a single, long fat crystal. It made a good light.

I asked Cassandra, "What is my purpose? What am I to accomplish?"

"That will be known to you in time," she said.

She left the arch and became a slender wraith-like spirit with very long, flowing blond hair. She was beautiful in that form, and I again told her so. She thanked me, and I followed her.

We were now on the floor of a valley, and it appeared to be the desert southwest. We came to an Indian couple. The man was working with hides, the woman was weaving a blanket. The blanket was red trimmed, there were diamond shapes set up in a pyramid style, and gray was in the middle. Cassandra stayed out of eyesight, but I knew she was there.

The couple were young, about mid-twenties. They were dressed traditionally. The camp was set up in front of a teepee with typical Plains Indian trappings. There was a fire. She wore a dark tan buckskin dress with intricate beadwork on the bodice and across the shoulder, the colors were blue, yellow, and white. The fringe on her sleeves was very long. Her hair was braided.

She turned to me and said, "Hello."

"Hello," I responded.

Do you have any questions?" she asked.

"I do," I said. "Why do I always feel fear? I was feeling some just before."

"I know that," the woman said. "It will be taken care of." She studied my face and nodded. "We will help you with that fear. You will overcome it." She then began transforming and became a white buffalo.

I said, "Wow, White Buffalo Woman."

The buffalo, transformed to a male, knelt before me, and said, "Get on."

I grabbed onto his mane and climbed on. He was soft, his fur was soft, and I blended in with him, and it felt comfortable. Cassandra now joined us, floating off to the left. We galloped at a high speed across the desert floor, dust rising behind us. It was so exhilarating.

When we stopped, I asked, "When will my fear be taken care of?"

"Be patient," Buffalo said and snorted, "Anna, you are always trying to make things happen. You want it right now. It will come to you. You must relax and go with the natural flow. You are on the right path."

At that point I asked, "You're taking me back now, aren't you?"

"Yes," he said. "You've done enough this time."

Then a beaded pipe with fringe floated into my hands. I examined it on all sides, touched by its lovely intricate design.

"This is a gift to you from me," Buffalo said.

Thrilled, I said, "Thank you. I can use this during my morning ceremonies."

We moved on, and I began to smell sage, which was the shaman's signal that we were coming to the end of the journey. We arrived at the entrance of the cave.

"Goodbye, Cassandra," I said. "Please thank the couple for me."

Then she was gone. Buffalo and I stepped out onto a ledge and looked at the valley below. I had gotten off him, and we stood side by side. It was a beautiful cloudless day. I saw a mountain with a road winding up to the summit. The sun shone on the road and glistened like a stream caught in sunlight.

"I want to go up there," I said. Even though I knew I probably wasn't supposed to.

"You're going up there, aren't you?" Buffalo said.

"Yes," I said. "There is probably plenty of time."

We had just started when the drums ended, and the Shaman told me to breathe deep and I reluctantly returned.

Anna had quickly engaged in the journey process and acquired allies. Cassandra is a guide at this point and Buffalo is a male ally with power. Note that the Plains Indian woman transformed into the male aspect White Buffalo, who is indeed her power ally. This is also an alchemical concept of Cuniunctio, the union of opposites, which will be discussed in more detail later.

Chapter 5

Spider and the Baby

When we met for Anna's next session, she appeared nervous, anxious, and fidgety. She could not identify the reason but did acknowledge those feelings.

I reminded her to rely on her allies and to summon others as needed. And that with her allies she could deal with any situation she would encounter. Our discussion reassured her, and we proceeded into the Journey space. I knew something of major significance was about to be revealed, and her report of her journey session did not disappoint.

Anna's Third Journey

The deep low beat of the drum began, building, filling the room, filling my body. Vibrations throbbed through me, over me, lifting me, carrying me away. The steady pulsing rhythm lifted me up to the Chalk Caves and my cave.

I approached my cave slowly and with great reluctance because I knew what I needed to do.

Upon going in, Cassandra was immediately there. I didn't have to call for her. She was in an intense, bright light form. I said, "Hello," and then I saw White Buffalo running up the incline. Thrilled to see him, I ran the short distance to where he had stopped and hugged him. I then climbed on his back. When I saw him, I said, "You are my power animal."

He said, "Yes, of course I am."

I was very nervous, apprehensive, I could feel my stomach tied in knots, knowing what I was going to do.

I told Cassandra and Buffalo that I needed to go to the arch. Buffalo took me there, but Cassandra wasn't along. My intentions were being relayed without anything being said or thought.

At the arch, I asked, "Is this what I really should do now?"

The answer was an emphatic yes.

"I knew it is," I said. But it was going to take a lot of courage, and I wasn't sure I could. Yet, I wanted to know about my baby. "Cassandra," I called, "Will you take me to my baby?" I needed to know what had happened to it.

We started out, but Cassandra wasn't with us. The way was dark, and my resolve began to fade. I saw some light rays from my first journey floating above me, and then White Buffalo Woman was beside me.

"I need courage," I said. "I want to complete this."

"You will have enough courage to do it and to keep going," she said. "Your allies are with you."

The fear I felt before she appeared had been

causing me to feel nauseous, my stomach now calmed somewhat, and we moved on. Buffalo and I entered the spiral tunnel from my first journey. The sides were lit, and it seemed to be turning, but it didn't affect us.

"Buffalo, shouldn't we have more help?"

"You have all the courage and help you need."

Then there were babies on each side and Cassandra appeared. "I look after the babies."

"Can I see mine, if it's here?"

She was once again gone, but there was an infant in front of me. I knew it was my baby, a girl. I picked her up and began to cuddle her, but she slowly became a huge, black spider and began to crawl up my shoulder into my hair. I was scared. I could feel the legs on my skin.

I didn't know what to do. "Let's get out of here, fast," I said.

Buffalo began to run, and we were out on an open plain. Wind flattened Buffalo's fur and blew in my face. Spider's legs blew in the wind too, and it seemed to disappear into the wind. A soft, black fur cloak draped across my shoulders in place of Spider.

The drumming stopped, but I knew I had to continue. I couldn't go back without completing my task. Images briefly materialized. One was a large eagle-like bird that had a black head and white body. My pipe also appeared briefly.

I again went to where my baby was but didn't need to go through the spiral tunnel. I was going to enter another cavern. I knew I was close to the child and the opening when these ghostly, frightening creatures appeared, about four or five. They floated around us. I remember the one in the front especially. It was spindly, the legs, arms, and the body, with two black holes for eyes and a craggy opening for a mouth. It was a pale green, muddy brown. They floated around us; a couple dived at us. I wanted to run but didn't. I stood my ground. I thought about using my crystal as a light saber if I needed it.

"I will not be stopped from seeing my child and talking to her."

These creatures then disappeared, and the child floated into my arms. This time I held her close, and she smiled at me. I was now able to nurse her. I put her to my right breast, and she suckled. Then she smiled at me, cooing and gurgling. She fell asleep, and I began to walk away. I still wasn't feeling as if I had completed my task though and knew there was more work ahead.

A three-year-old child appeared. She smiled at me and said, "Mommy, I love you and I forgive you." We walked on and a fourteen-year-old appeared. She said, "Mommy, I love you and I forgive you."

Then, Cassandra appeared.

I asked her, "Who are you?" And Buffalo stopped.

"You know," she answered.

"Could that really be, or do I just want it to be?"

"I am your child. I forgive you. I was needed here to be your guide when you would decide to do this."

I stretched out my arms to her, and she entered them. Then a bright, white light engulfed all three of us and spread through my body, warming me all the way through. When the light cleared, I looked up and saw rays of sun, black and white feathers floated down. They settled on my shoulders in a beautiful cloak. Cassandra was there in a dazzling light form.

"Buffalo, we need to hurry," I said. "It's almost time to be back."

We rushed toward the entrance. I jumped off Buffalo and came back.

Anna had carried the weight of guilt for an abortion for so many years. She was finally able to face this demon and, with the help of her allies, conquer it and free herself from that burden. The allies are those aspects of our psyche we all possess but fail to acknowledge and utilize. The ghostly figures were her fear manifested. Spider that clung to her was the guilt she had carried for so many years into adulthood.

These troublesome emotions are the demons that inhabit our psychic world in that they can be a crippling burden that affects our lives in a multitude of ways and can remain with us during our entire life span.

But, in addition to these demons, our spiritual makeup consists of their counterparts, our allies of courage, wisdom, magic, strength: all the characteristics of the hero that enable one to effect transformation. One simply must call up this latent energy as needed to initiate the healing process.

Anna transcended linear time, entering the nonlinear realm. In healing the past, she heals her present and her future. Anna transformed Spider (guilt) into a soft, black fur cloak draped across her shoulders. In addition, she received forgiveness from her aborted child and again was wrapped in a beautiful, feathered cloak.

Chapter 6

The Dark Side

Our discussion prior to this session centered on Spider and how to deal with this dark entity. In previous encounters she ran to escape, which afforded her temporary safety. I informed her she will have to confront this demon and vanquish it. If not, it will return. I reminded her to call on her allies and to burn, bury, or throw any remains into water. I explained that these actions are alchemical operations related to transformation. Anna expressed fear but felt increased confidence in her allies and herself.

Anna's Fourth Journey

I was eager to begin. When we "relaxed and meditated," I was already at the cave and wanted to go in. When there I saw my arch and some stalagmites and stalactites. The arch shone very white and gleaming against the duller, smoky white of the mites and tites.

I entered the cave and found White Buffalo waiting for me. He seemed larger than before, but every bit as white and beautiful with a massive head. He snorted with power and impatience letting me know he was ready as well. I got on his back.

Cassandra was not around. I called for her, and she came briefly. We went to the arch, and then she left.

"Buffalo," I said. "We have quite a bit to accomplish. We will need White Buffalo Woman."

Spider showed itself at the arch, and I knew I would soon have to face it. I thought about trying it this time but didn't feel ready.

I again called for White Buffalo Woman after moving away from the arch and leaving Spider behind. She appeared.

I told her what I needed to do, and said, "I am going to need a lot of courage and help from a warrior."

She led us to the Indian village. Many tepees stood beside a stream in a grove of trees. Five warriors rode out to greet us.

"These warriors will accompany us," she said.

We rode across a plain, up a slope, and back down. Buffalo and I led the way.

We came to a series of doors and windows, and finally entered the bathroom of the apartment I had lived in when I got pregnant. The claw-footed tub was the prominent feature. It was here, while bathing, that I made my decision.

Spider showed itself, coming around from the back of the tub. I had a crystal in my hand, and it became a light saber. I stabbed at the demon, hitting it. Nothing seemed to happen. Now a warrior appeared to my left, but he was not very effective. I used some hacking swings. Spider moved back. The thing grew to the size of an adult sea turtle. Finally, after some sparring, I speared it in the middle, but it still didn't die. I lifted it in the air, its legs thrashing while impaled on the saber.

I began to think I would never be able to kill this dark creature. Then the warrior speared it and freed it from my saber. I hacked at it. I hacked and hacked, and finally chopped it up into hundreds of small pieces.

A frog appeared, a large one, and ate some of Spider. I thought that was good but wanted to see it washed away in water. A stream had been flowing next to our battlefield. The warrior and I shoved all the hacked parts into it. I watched for a long time, until every piece of that demon floated away.

We then returned to the business of retrieving my baby. At the cavern there were many more of the creatures than before. Not one of them made any threatening moves, however, and I wasn't afraid of them. I asked if we could enter their realm and they said yes. They rose as if they were a curtain. I looked up and there were hundreds of them floating above us. I could see sunlight filtering past them.

Inside the cavern, Cassandra waited.

"Can I take the baby back with me?"

She said, "You can." And she stepped aside.

"Thank you." I got the sense we were saying goodbye on another level.

I once again passed many babies before I came to mine. I picked her up and hugged her. I had gotten off Buffalo. He stood very close.

I let her nurse, then asked, "Do you want to come back with me?" I showed her a rose quartz stone I had with me that my grandson, her nephew, had given me. I asked, "Would you like to come back in it?"

She indicated yes, she would and entered the stone I held in my hand. I placed it carefully in my medicine bag.

The warrior was no longer with me. I left riding Buffalo. We were now going through open country and then climbing. I realized we were on the winding road going up the mountain I had seen on my second journey. I looked out from where we were and thought I saw closely growing trees. They were very thick. On closer examination I realized they were a gigantic herd of buffalo. We were in the sky now. We rode into the middle of this herd. They allowed us to pass, peacefully parting before us. I felt they were welcoming us. The feeling was fantastic.

I wanted to play but could sense the end of the Journey. Buffalo galloped to the mouth of the cave where I hopped off. I thanked everyone quickly and returned. I wanted to laugh and joke. It was playtime.

———

Anna's exuberance on return told me she had accomplished her task. Her excitement on recounting the battle with Spider was animated with gestures and utterances as if she was reenacting the scene. I informed her she had become a warrior, which pleased her to no end. She was ready to take on any challenge. I counseled her to be wary of confrontation now, as warriors pick and choose their battles, and most battles are not worthy of their energy. Choose wisely.

The alchemical process *Solutio* was introduced in this Journey when Anna hacked up the spider, and she and the warrior put its parts into the stream and washed it away.

Chapter 7

Shaman's Worldview

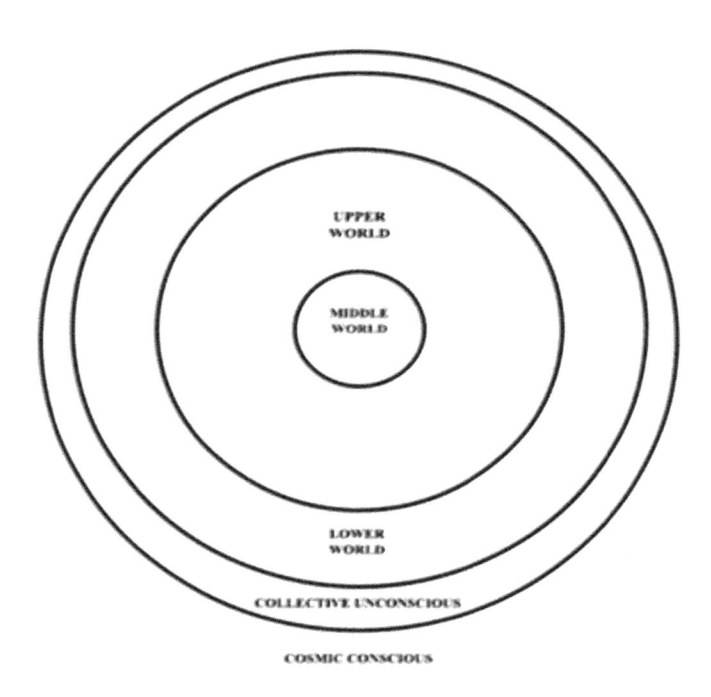

Figure 1

The shamanic worldview corresponds with the Western perspective of consciousness. The ego or conscious state is a middle world shamanic state. Upper and lower worlds are relegated to the subconscious and unconscious states. Beyond is the shamanic connection to the cosmos.

We Westerners stumble blindly into the twenty-first century and look askance at the age-old meditative practices of the East. We frown on those who practice meditation as hippies, oddballs, or just weird people. The portrayals of indigenous spiritual practitioners are of a dancing rattle-waving madman. What is not taken into consideration is that these practitioners have centuries of tested and proven methodologies, whereas the Western approach is in its infancy and relies on the ever-growing array of drugs to treat a spiritually wounded society. It is most often the spirit that requires healing, not the body that houses the spirit.

I speak of spirit not in the religious framework but in the sense of that which is alive within us. But that is not to say that religious beliefs and faith does not enter this process. When it does, one gains a more profound understanding and appreciation of their faith because they experience it at a more personal level. Shamanism is not an organized religion. It is a methodology practiced throughout the world for centuries, for the purpose of healing of self or others and expanding consciousness in the process of individuation.

The shamanic experience is one of ever-expanding consciousness. It is said that people use only a small percentage of the brain's potential. It is also said that consciousness is relegated to the brain. It is a component of the system that creates the experience of consciousness. The contributions of all the senses, the various other bodily systems, experiences, beliefs, values, training, and so much more define and create that experience. What is limited is the potential use of the range of the consciousness experience.

Figure 1 is a model of shamanic consciousness. At its core is the middle world, the ego state that the uninitiated walk around in daily. When an individual practices meditation, it can be said they are in a subconscious realm. The unconscious state, the lower world, is seldom entered except in the dream state. And although it is the repository of one's entire life experience, it is as an abandoned dusty warehouse. Yet therein lays the treasure.

Then there is the collective unconscious. We identify and belong to groups that share values, ideas, social, and cultural beliefs. Shamans, by whatever name, occur in every culture in the world. They are the psychiatrist, psychologist, social worker, artist, and minister of the community. Though separated by distance and geography they all share this same worldview and employ the same practices and techniques.

Beyond that is cosmic consciousness. There Shamans engage atoms and particles, much like quantum physicists, in search of understanding energy, the gods, and the source of all that exists.

The shamanic journey is the practice of expanding consciousness, at will, into these realms for the purposes of healing, gaining knowledge, and empowering our spiritual selves.

With the guidance of a knowledgeable Shaman, the practitioner learns not only how to navigate these realms but also learns the art of transformation, one of the keys to affecting change. This is the mythical Hero's Journey that Joseph Campbell refers to in his many narratives. It is the search for Self, the process of Individuation.

Chapter 8

Descent, the Shamanic Journey

When did my foot first tread onto the path? There is no way to know that for sure. There are events and circumstances, studies and practices that have shaped and molded the man and the Shaman that I now see as being instrumental in preparing me for this place on my journey.

One of those circumstances is the years spent in a maximum-security institution working among the criminally insane. The lessons learned were hard won but critical to survival in that world. To let down one's guard meant exposing one's underbelly to spiritual carnivores in a place where chinks and cracks are constantly searched for and tested daily. It served as a training ground for learning about energies of various colorings, and how to protect one's energy field. In that world, demons roamed unfettered whispering fouled-breath obscenities into undefended ears that the inmates harken to as if to angels.

The place on the path I am at now is not one I would have imagined years ago. The practice of Shamanism did not come to me as fire spit from the heavens but manifested in degrees, some small, others in quantum leaps. Teachers found their way into my life in the form of books. Despite the controversy associated with Carlos Castaneda and accusations of misleading material, he described concepts of reality that provided me with mirrors to hold up to my own. Others such as Stanislav Grof, Mircea Eliade, Michael Harner, and so many others have added pieces to the puzzle. I rode, and continue to ride, a wave of practice initiated by the ancestors like a drop of rain in a shallow puddle that became a ripple and finally a tide awash in my global consciousness. And the lesson gleaned along the way is that there is no reaching the destination, only the journey and what we have learned while treading on that path.

Having worked and studied in the field of psychiatry for decades, I have witnessed every form of treatment utilized to treat the spiritually wounded from A to Z. Every form of "mental illness" has passed before me during this extended period of apprenticeship, and I've worked with the finest psychiatrists and psychologists in a university setting. The Western approach has been to treat symptoms with medications. And generally, the symptoms have subsided temporarily, but the cause of the symptoms is rarely treated. In addition, the side effects of treatment are, many times, untenable for the patient and often physically damaging.

Meditative practices introduced me to deeper states of consciousness, and university studies in world religions revealed the many methods practiced throughout the world. The use of various plants is as valid an application as meditation. Presently, the use of Ayahuasca, a psychoactive potion indigenous to the Amazon rain forest, has found its way to the shores of California and is spreading throughout the United States as a portal to the spiritual experience. Ayahuasqueros, highly trained Shamans, guide participants into a spirit world where they discover their own connection to the spirits that dwell there.

Expanded states of consciousness are the doorway to the Shaman's Journey, where participants engage the fanciful entities and vaporous edifices that inhabit the lower world. These entities are real, and can best be described as psychic energy, in that they interact or interfere with one's daily existence. Historically, Shamans have employed psychoactive plants in their practice, recognizing the power and importance of altering or utilizing expanded states of consciousness to empower, heal, or gain knowledge beyond ordinary consciousness.

Historical tales such as Homer's *Ulysses* and Dante's *Inferno* tell of mythic journeys that are metaphors of the Shaman's Journey. In them, heroes leave the safety of everyday life and set out on a quest. Along the way the hero is tested and confronted by difficult trials and dangers. If the hero is able to overcome these, he will be rewarded with the object of his quest and earn the right to return home to take his rightful place or claim his prize. That is equally true of the hero undertaking the Shaman's Journey. Myths are metaphorical in nature and stand the test of time. They can be understood and recognized by the Shaman and scholar of such arcane knowledge.

Chapter 9

A Treasure Map

The first duty of the Shaman Guide is to prepare the journeyer for the adventure. Job one for the journeyer is the acquisition of spiritual allies. It is these allies that will negotiate the journeyer's passage through unknown landscapes.

It is imperative to engage allies as they are essential in the Journeyer's process. Without allies one is psychically naked, without the needed help to encounter the unknown. The four primary allies recommended are only a few of the infinite possibilities. Aided by these four allies one can encounter and deal with any situation that arises out of the descent into the labyrinth of consciousness. These allies can manifest themselves in any form they choose, from animals to people, inanimate objects, a sword, or as an energy felt by the journeyer. Such allies will be referred to as entities.

The first ally is a guide to take the journeyer to the lower world and to guide the return. Without a guide, one may wander in the void without direction. The journey should always be motivated by purpose and intent, and a guide will assist in that intention. Initially, the purpose is to experience the Shaman's Journey, acquire the four primary allies, and encounter sanctuary, a place of safety, of peace, a place where one can retreat whenever necessary.

The second ally is one of courage, for obvious reasons.

The third ally is for protection from anything that feels threatening to the journeyer.

Power, physical power is the fourth ally. Should one encounter a demon, and it is highly likely that this will occur, an ally with physical power will be useful. Personal power is acquired when one faces the demons, battles them, and vanquishes them. Several allies can be manifested within a single entity. A power ally may also serve as an ally for protection, and both will manifest in a form unique to each journeyer.

Other allies will manifest as needed to guide, advise, teach, inform, promote growth, and facilitate the spiritual transformative and healing processes. Allies cannot be acquired from a book or by personal preference. They can only be acquired through spiritual practices.

Procedurally, and ideally, a quiet, comfortable, darkened room is set aside for journey and ritual. Journeyers are provided with information they may need to facilitate the process and told what to expect during the ceremony in preparation for the journey.

The space used is smudged with sage, and a brief ceremony is performed to create sacred ground. The mechanics of the ceremony may differ with each practitioner. What remains constant is the intent to create sacred ground for spiritual practice. Also, the journeyer wants to leave his body on sacred ground so that the spirit can journey freely, knowing the body is attended by the Shaman.

That ceremony completed, the journeyer lies down and is made comfortable. The journeyer is covered with a warm blanket, then a relaxation process occurs, and shamanic drumming begins. When the journeyer is ready, he will begin visualizing an opening, a doorway or passage to the lower world. If the journeyer feels ready, he will enter the opening and begin the descent. It is at this point that the journeyer has ventured into the realm of spirits, dragons, magicians, demons, and other seemingly fantastical phenomena. But once experienced, the initiate cannot resist the lure of the underworld or the quest for the treasure they are sure is hidden there awaiting their return. Any discoveries made earlier are clues to even greater discoveries.

Chapter 10

The Great Master of Ecstasy

C.G. Jung, Master Shaman, and many others revealed the inner workings of Shamanism in such detail and clarity that it is relatively easy to find comprehensive works on the subject. Any practicing Shaman reading these works will find their world revealed and spread out before them as a feast laid out in unparalleled bounty. The recognition in their works of the complexity of Shamanism's many aspects are undeniable and profound. Therefore, I will refer to their contributions as related to the shamanic experience throughout this text.

Cuniunctio

There is an incident of soul retrieval at the beginning of this upcoming journey segment, and an example of the union of opposites following that account. Both are a movement toward wholeness or integrating a fragmented spirit.

Anna's Fourth Journey (Cont'd)

Leaving the stream, we entered deeper into the cave. We were stopped by six ghostly, frightening creatures at a junction in the tunnel. (Note: It is a junction, a place to make a choice, and she names the nature of the creatures, fear.) They floated around us, a couple dived at us, and we ducked. Before we knew it, they left, leaving us feeling anxious.

We entered a large cavern, dimly lit and damp smelling, and at the far end found a baby. Wrapped as it was, I did not recognize it for what it was until it wriggled and emitted a squall. l then I knew it to be my baby. I took the child in my arms and hugged her to my breasts.

I asked, "Would you like to come back with me?" I had a stone in my medicine bag given to me by my daughter. I showed the stone to the baby and asked, "Can you enter this?" She somehow indicated she could and became a brilliant white light and melded with the stone I now held in my palm. The stone felt quite warm in my hand. I placed it once again in my medicine bag, and I brought it out with me.

I thanked White Buffalo Woman and asked to go to the warrior village. "I need to thank them," I said, "especially one, for the help in defeating Spider and rescuing my infant self."

At the village, I found the five warriors and thanked them. I asked, "Which one of you helped me defeat and destroy Spider?"

A warrior stepped forward; his hair hung unbraided past his shoulders. His chest was bare, and he wore buckskin pants.

"Thank you for your help."

As we spoke clouds formed around our feet,

and we began to rise from the earth. An eagle waited for us in the upper world, and asked, "Where do you wish to go?"

"To the moon," I said, and we were whisked there. We sat on the surface of the moon, looking into space and at Earth. I reached out and touched my home planet. My hand passed through it. The warrior caught a star and gave it to me. Then Eagle returned us to the Earth.

Eagle deposited us beside a stream glistening in the noonday sun. The warrior took my hand and led me into the water. Instead of being cold, it felt warm and pleasant. We followed the stream to a waterfall and stood under its cascading waters. I became aware of my wet clothes clinging to my body. The closeness of the handsome warrior was having an effect on me. He reached out and touched one of my breasts; his touch sent tingling waves through me. His hands moved to the buttons of my blouse, which he adeptly unbuttoned. His dexterity with the snap and zipper of my jeans was just as efficient, and he had my outer garments removed and tossed carelessly aside. There was no fumbling as he unsnapped my lacy, white bra and slid the straps off my shoulders. His hands slid down my ribs, creating a weakness in them, making it difficult to stand. I stepped out of the flimsy garment and kicked it aside. The water cooled my hot skin but did nothing to quell the fires he had ignited.

He made short work of removing his own garments. The leggings and breech cloth tossed aside beside my own twentieth century clothes. He began washing my body, rubbing water over my skin. I realized this was a ritual cleansing, a celebration of our victory. I washed his body as well.

He took my hand and led me to the small cave behind the falls. The water provided a curtain offering a cool sanctuary. He laid me gently in the shallow water at the back of the cave and lay next to me. He kissed first one breast, then the other, and gently licked my erect nipples. His lips did not rest but moved over my body, adding fuel to the fire. The roar of the waterfall muffled my screams as he brought our love making to completion.

As I mentioned prior to the journey above, Anna experienced a soul retrieval, like we've seen in previous journeys, when she got in contact with her baby and convinced her to enter the stone to return with her. In that way the baby became a part of Anna's medicine bundle.

While in the cave behind the waterfall, she engaged in a cleansing process that is an alchemical operation of *Solutio* or a water-related operation important in the transformative stages and is considered the root of alchemy.

Finally, she engages the warrior in sexual union. Anna's male and female aspects are joined to form a completed whole, *Cuniunctio,* which is a goal of individuation. It is clarified when she states, "He brought our love making to completion."

Chapter 11

In Search of Merlin's Sword

Mythology plays an enduring role in the life of the Shaman, and more likely in everyone's life. That it is not recognized or acknowledged is a monumental loss to contemporary society. But as one traverses the path to enlightenment, to personal growth in search of the Self, myth begins to manifest in wondrous ways unexpected by the searcher. The myths are played out in shadow and in public arenas. In a brilliant impulse of creative genius, filmmaker George Lucas called on Joseph Campbell to provide inspiration for one of the most iconoclastic films of the century, *Star Wars*. Its popularity and quality speak to that which resonates in us at the deepest level of our consciousness.

Many times, a version of an ancient myth appears in our lives. As Jung would suggest we need to focus on what these myths are because they have a major impact on who we are and where we are in our life stages. Below is an example of a classic myth followed by how it appeared in my life.

The legend of King Arthur and the sword is a well-known and enduring story. As with most mythological narratives it endures the test of time. It touches a place within us that reaches back into time and connects us to our shared ancestry and to shared experiences. The wizard Merlin is said to have created a sword using magic and inserted it into an anvil on a large stone, or in some accounts, into the stone itself. Arthur, taken at birth and raised by

Merlin, was the son of the then king, Uther Pendragon. Uther died with no known heirs. Merlin intervened and decreed that, "Who so pulleth out this sword of this stone is the right wise born king of all England." Of course, all the contenders for the throne tried and failed. Arthur, pulled the sword, claimed his right and authority to be king of England. This sword is not to be confused with Excalibur, which is a sword given to Arthur by the "Lady of the Lake" to defeat his enemies. But in both instances the sword is the symbol of authority and power. Arthur goes on to restore order and prosperity to the kingdom.

It is a scientific fact that quartz crystals vibrate at a constant rate when an electrical current is introduced. It was his premise that all minerals have a unique vibrational property and that these vibrational properties could be used to effect changes in the body when applied. His search led him to experiment with a combination of stones fastened together in a complex configuration related to their vibrational properties to form these tools.

I became a test subject for one of these healing tools. Hank Smith presented me with one of the healing tools he had constructed which consisted of a large quartz crystal attached to a base made of amethyst. A variety of gems and minerals adorned the crystal to further enhance the energy of the healing tool, all of which were interconnected by copper wiring.

Instructed to close my eyes and hold this tool with both hands I was to simply allow or register any sensations that would arise during this time. After a brief period of relaxation and clearing of my mind, the initial sensation was the coolness of the stones and the shape, its angular lines, and its weight. My mind drifted and then a mental image of a dagger appeared out of nowhere. I lost all sensation of holding the wand. On closer examination, I noted that the blade of the dagger was a bright silver double-edged metal, and the tip had a barb on both edges that looked quite dangerous. The handle gleamed gold in color and had a black stone inlay with a blue lapis lazuli tip that curved slightly.

As I studied it, a message came to me. "This blade can only be forged by the hands of a man with a pure heart. It is a ceremonial tool, powerfully dangerous, and finally, its meaning will be made clear with time."

I drifted again and then returned to the table where I sat with Hank Smith watching. I reported to him that I had not really felt anything I could discern as a different sensation. I related the vision I had of the dagger. He nodded his head knowingly but did not say anything. Later, I did record the event in my journal with a sketch of the dagger. The event held little information and passed with no particular significance to me at that time.

Several months later, the wife of Hank Smith had planned a trip to Kansas to see her parents. She invited my wife and me to join her. We both declined, but then later I decided I wanted to go as I had some free time and would enjoy the getaway.

Driving and chatting, my companion began to talk about her father. His name was Henry, the same as her husband, both were called Hank. She spoke of her father, Hank Bradly, in general and in endearing terms. With pride she spoke of how he was not only a deacon in a church but also a machinist, a blacksmith, and made knives of extraordinary beauty and precision as an avocation. And then she capped this off with the statement, "He is one of the few men I know with a pure heart."

At that moment, the vision of the dagger returned, my heart skipped a beat, and I felt detached from my surroundings. My mind churned and then I had a moment of clarity. The reason for my present journey to Kansas was because a wizard with a pure heart lived there. I was on my way to pay a visit to the wizard with a request.

Prior to this I had been thinking: Where am I going to find a blacksmith who knew about forging steel? What were the odds that I would find someone who could create an item of this caliber? And what are the odds of finding a man with a pure heart who could forge steel?

As we drove, I created a more complete sketch of this dagger and could think of little else. Questions and uncertainties crept into my mind. What would I say to him? What if he declined my request? We arrived in midafternoon and pulled up to a Kansas-style farmhouse and were greeted by several friendly dogs then her father and mother. The family resemblance was there and after greetings and embraces, we were invited in and fed. All along all I could think of was my request.

Finally, sometime later, my companion asked her father to show me his work. He led me to another house nearby, smaller, and cluttered. Upon entering, I found it full of machines and tools of all sorts. From a drawer, he extracted several knives he had made. Each one was a work of art, beautifully executed. After exploring the shop and hearing about his process, I finally had the courage to inquire if he would consider my request to forge the dagger for me. I would gladly pay his asking price for this work.

I showed him the sketch, and he studied it for a few minutes. I could see the gears turning in his head, and after several minutes of waiting, felt sure he would decline.

"I would have to make a special tool, but yeah I can do that," he said.

My heart sang and I felt elated. After spending more time with him, I realized that my concerns had been groundless as there was no way he could have declined the challenge presented him. The only instruction I gave him was to feel free to use his own discretion in creating this piece.

He then led me to a collection of old and large metal farm

files. After examining these, he chose one and handed it to me. My only thought was, how in the world would he be able to forge this chunk of metal into that magnificent sword?

Approximately six weeks later, I received some photos of him holding the blade. The old file extended out from a silver blade as if it had grown there, transformed. He informed me he still had to create the handle and would then be done with it. Not long after that Hank Bradly arrived in Loveland to visit his daughter and her husband, Hank Smith, and had with him the completed piece except for the stone inlays, and he then related to me that it was more of a short sword than a dagger. The sword set my heart to thrumming; it was indeed one of a kind and beautiful.

The wizard then proceeded to provide me information regarding the forging of steel and the proper care of this piece. I received more information about forging steel than I believed I would ever need or use, only to be proven disastrously wrong at a later date.

Initially, I had thought to have the stone inlays made by Hank Smith, the stone sculptor. I then decided he had done his part in this process and that it needed some feminine energy. My wife had traveled to Oregon the year before and had brought back some black rainbow obsidian. A few days after seeing it, I knew it had to be the inlay for the sword. I took the obsidian to a woman who owned a rock and mineral shop not far from where I lived. She agreed to complete the inlays. When she had finished with the inlays, I retrieved it from her. Holding the completed sword in my hands, the emotions that arose were intense. The inlays were beautifully done, and the purple rainbow sheen of the obsidian shone like fire. I understood then that she too was a person with a pure heart.

The sword had indeed been drawn from the stone tool created by Hank Smith, ironically a black man or the black Smith.

The second wizard Hank Bradly lived far away and required that I set out on a quest to find him. That he knew how to forge steel, could create such an item, and was a man with a pure heart is beyond coincidence. The Arthurian Legend states that the creator of that legendary sword died so that no other swords could be created. It was to be one of a kind.

Rainbow obsidian and lapis lazuli. The energy of Lapis Lazuli is said to support anyone ready to step into their power and authentic self.

Shortly after delivering the sword to me, Hank Bradly's daughter called me with tragic news. Her father had died of a heart attack. His wife reported that he had worked feverishly on this piece to get it done. This piece was his final and best work.

The wizard of Kansas with the unfinished sword blade.

To make matters even more complex, Hank Smith also died, shortly after Hank Bradly, also of a heart attack. The legend of Merlin's sword replayed itself out in glorious and tragic detail. The sword is an extraordinary one-of-a-kind mythical piece.

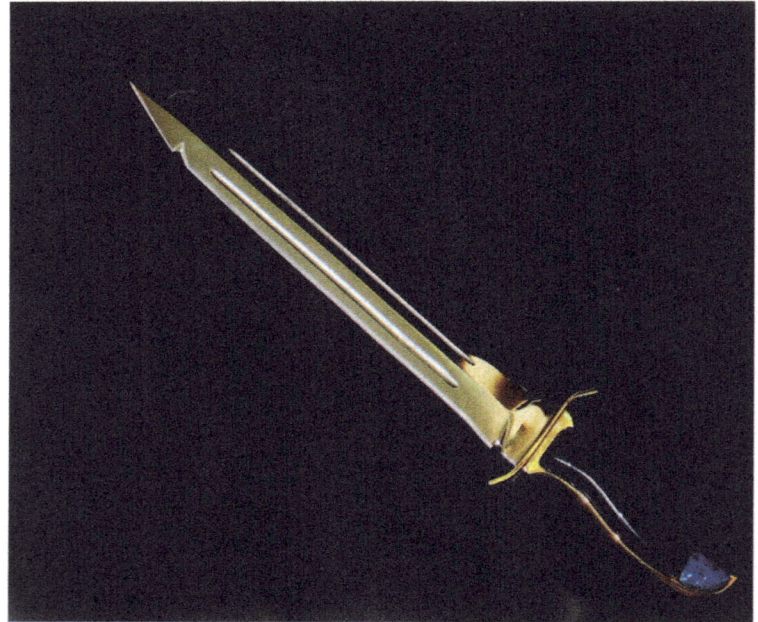

The sword restored after many years wrapped hidden on a shelf.

Chapter 12

Death and Myth

One purpose myth serves, then, is to provide meaning to the life experience. Such meaning, however, is deeper and more encompassing than merely intellectual understanding. It is rather a living meaning, relevant to the heart and to the spirit, as much as to the mind, to be conveyed through painting, dance, music, poetry, and literature, and not just through rational discourse and theories. As a culture, we are lacking a collective myth that can put us in touch with this deeper level of meaning, and we see the consequences reflected in all manner of social and psychological ills. "Meaninglessness," Jung wrote in his autobiography, "inhibits the fullness of life and is therefore equivalent to illness." If you are not living a fully meaningful life, such that you feel vitally connected to the numinous wellsprings of the psyche, then it is likely you are not living out of your full power. In such a scenario, you could become psychologically or even physically sick, since the life power that you should be experiencing and expressing as a positive force, instead, finds expression unconsciously, and manifests in a destructive form. For this reason, it is important, perhaps even imperative, to have a guiding myth or life philosophy that helps you to draw upon and express everything you are, such that you can pour your full being into your life, affirming joy and suffering alike.

In many myths, for example, one finds the idea that the god or the hero dies and is resurrected, reborn into a different form. This theme is evident in myths of Osiris, Attis, Adonis, Persephone, Dionysus, Mithras, Jesus, and others. It is also intrinsic to shamanic mythology. The Shaman afflicted by a mysterious spiritual illness, embarks on an initiatory descent into the underworld of the spirits, which typically involving an encounter with death. He then returns to the daylight world, transformed and transfigured, able then to serve as a guide and healer for the community.

The role of mythology plays a vital part of the development of the Shaman as well as the journeyer. At each stage of development, myth plays itself out in relationship to the level or necessity of the process.

Looking back on the story of the Cat in the opening pages, one sees several instances of this process. In vision one Cat appeared in response to the first early experience of death of an aunt. In that instance a crude manifestation of the sword (an old, long, rusty knife) revealed itself, but the recipient was not at an appropriate level of development for a true sword. The result was that Cat fell away but was not vanquished and was relegated to the depths of the psyche.

Many years later during the second vision the stage of development was more advanced. During this manifestation the response was not one of fight but of flight, which was more appropriate at that point. Again, Cat was still not vanquished and was relegated to the depths of obscurity.

Cat again manifests several years later. As a result of self-examination, questing, seeking, study, and practice, Cat (death) was accepted. That fear of death was transformed into power of equal strength, and Cat became a power ally. Once again one can see alchemy at work and the transformative nature of the experience. Further illustrating how Alchemy involves operations that result in transformations that occur during a lifetime in pursuit of manifesting a higher self.

Chapter 13

The Anima

Author's Dream of 1996

I am sitting on the ground near a construction site. There is litter and construction material scattered about. I am speaking to someone and absentmindedly brushing dirt away from a white pebble buried in the ground before me. Note: The digging is a process of uncovering something. The construction site is also relevant.

As I brush, more of the white surface begins to emerge. When about four-square inches of the surface are exposed, I realize that it is bone and the top of a skull. The sutures of the skull are evident. I continue to dig it out, until I break into a cave.

There I find an entire skeleton seated in a meditative posture. The cave is about six feet wide, six feet deep, and not quite as high. An old wood frame, tied together with some type of fiber, stands above the figure and to the far edges of the cave. From this frame hangs an assortment of what appears to be pieces of tattered cloth and some plants or herbs. What are these old remnants?

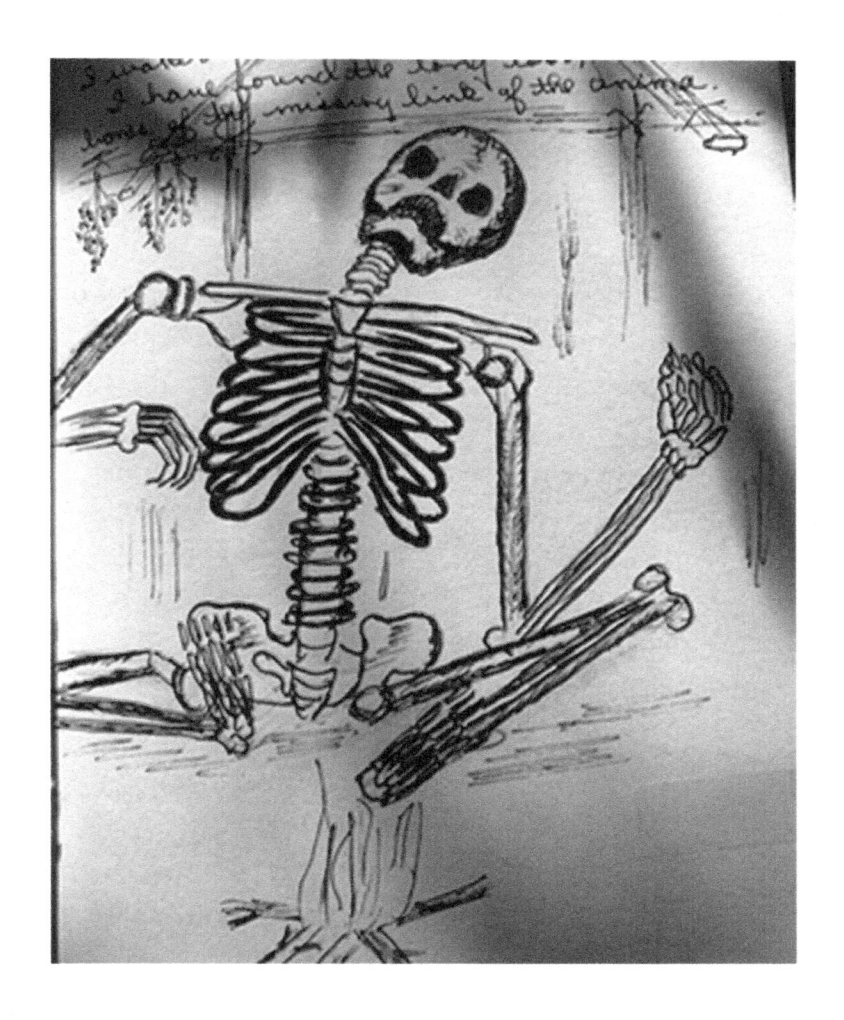

I understand that the skeleton is that of a female and that it is "the missing link," and is quite valuable, the oldest female bones ever found. People are gathering and are excited that I had made this discovery. Word spreads about this find, and people from universities and museums approach me to purchase it for study. I am offered one hundred thousand dollars and decline their offers.

Each succeeding offer is larger than the last. Yet, I refuse to sell. The offers reach two million dollars. At that point, I realize the missing link I have excavated is my Anima.

———◆———

The need here was to integrate the Anima or the operation of *Conunctio* to advance to a higher state. The concept of "going to one's bones" was obvious here and referred to the function of being stripped of one's ego self, looking at who we believe we are, and what flesh (persona)s we have hung on those bones.

The Strong Feminine Warrior: From the Cave Gallery sculpture collection.

Chapter 14

Sublimatio

Author's Dream of 2009

Kate, Helena, and I have been summoned to a castle, and we understand the call to be of great importance. We begin our passage on a narrow path wide enough for the three of us to walk side by side. The path leads through an ancient oak forest. Creaks and groans emanate from the trees as we make our way through our dimly lit surroundings. The forest is alive and aware of us passing through. The trees watch us and communicate with one another about where we are at on our path. A hawk follows us, keeping track of us as well. We have traveled a fair distance Through a break in the trees, we catch a glimpse of an ancient castle that stands on a rise of earth and at a distance from us. We arrive at a sharp bend in the trail and are confronted by a large, old, ornate, vault door. It reminds me of the old vault at the Bank of Denver. The vault door is a pale gold color with darker gold painted scroll works, large enough for a person to walk through.

It is in the forest where mystery and adventure lies in wait. Think of the many children's stories that involve a forest.

The forest is too thick to allow us to go around the vault door. We attempt to anyway, and the forest draws closer together to block our passage. We discuss the situation and conclude that we are meant to be challenged. We decide it is a test to determine if we are the people qualified or needed at the castle. It became clear that we are needed at the castle for an unknown reason.

We consider using dynamite, power tools, and other means to get the vault open so we can pass through. We try using various numbers on the lock without success. Finally, we realize we must use our knowledge, magical skills, and powers to get it open.

Kate approaches the vault and puts her hands on the dial, the latch wheel, and then the door. She then whispers something in my ear. I nod my head as if to say okay. I understand.

Helena produces an ancient leatherbound book. It is light brown and worn. The pages are tattered and yellowed. When she opens it, a musty smell rises from its pages. She thumbs through the pages, stops at one, reads it, her finger moving down the page, and then whispers something in my ear. I acknowledge what I am being told with an affirmative nod. She gives me information from three separate pages.

I stand for a moment looking at the vault, then approach it and reach out with both hands as if to put my hands on it. As I do so, I close my eyes. I expect to encounter the doors, but my hands pass through the metal. I can see it in my mind, the inner workings, the gears, and levers. I move certain levers that turn gears, and the door locks release with sounds like a hammer on an anvil. I withdraw and the three of us pull on the door. It is heavy and thick. We open it and pass through. I realize at this point that it is indeed a test, and we have succeeded. I awaken.

The safe is opened and whatever treasures are there are now available. The castle awaits further investigation.

As I mentioned earlier, Joseph Campbell, Shaman, recognized and conceptualized myths and alchemy into coherent and meaningful structures. These myths and stories help us to understand our nature by serving as a living history of how we have evolved over time and yet remain connected to that heritage. The Hero's Journey is the better known of his mythological concepts and is deeply engrained in the psyche of humanity. That is the primary aspect of Joseph Campbell's work that George Lucas incorporated in Star Wars with great success.

It begins with the call. One can respond to the call or not. But if one ignores the call the story cannot unfold, the treasure cannot be found, or the goal achieved. Upon answering the call, the hero's path leads quickly into the forest, which often represents the unconscious. It is alive and aware. It is in the forest where things happen, the mysterious and the unknown. One can disappear in the forest. It is removed from usual surroundings but has a life of its own. On entering the forest, it is evident one is leaving the usual behind and is venturing into another realm, where potential is in the wind and in the branches and beckons one deeper into its grasp. The leaves and vines brush against the traveler in intimate caresses, assuring, soothing. Step off the path and something catches your eye in a fleeting moment. The only way to know what it is, is to search it out and perhaps catch a glimpse that will draw the traveler deeper into its embrace. And there will be found dragons, trolls, witches, and magicians residing in caves and cottages and in the trees and the glens.

On examining dreams, one must first take note of the environment or scene of the dream's action. In many fairy tales it is the forest, dark and impenetrable to the eye, like deep water and the sea. It is the container of the unknown and the mysterious. It is synonymous with the unconscious. Trees are the living elements that make up the forest. Trees, like fishes in the water, represent the living contents of the unconscious. One tree is conspicuous for its great size. The oak is especially significant and stands out as separate yet a part of the whole. Trees have individuality. A tree can symbolize an aspect of personality. The ancient oak is a central figure in the forest among the contents of the unconscious, possessing personality in the most marked degree. It is the prototype of the Self, a symbol of the source and goal of the Individuation process. The oak stands for the still unconscious core of the personality, the plant symbolism indicating a state of deep unconsciousness.

The hawk in the dream, symbolizing a being of higher spirit, circles overhead, ever watchful, and present. Then, the ancient Castle in the distance reveals itself, the goal. There one might find a king and queen, the princess, knights, treasures, perhaps a magician, hidden knowledge, and just as likely dragons storming the walls of the fortress. Castles are enchanted with its mysteries, hidden doorways, dark corridors, and its pennants and towers. The Castle does guard its secrets, though, behind massive stone walls and turrets. Structures are important in that they represent and define themselves as mental constructs. A castle is significantly different than a hovel.

Arriving at the bend, a critical place on the journey, the old vault presents as an obstacle. What is found beyond vault doors? The door is gold in color, the alchemical equivalent of the alchemist's goal. The vault is guarding something of great value.

Even the forest colludes against us. We have determined we are being tested. We finally agree we must use our knowledge and magical skills to get it open. Kate, being an intuitive, places her hands on the vault and intuits certain information. Helena shares wisdom or knowledge from an ancient book. And both pass it on to me.

My hands pass through the outer steel and the inner workings appear in my mind. I manipulate the gears and levers and the door locks release in heavy metallic concert. To manipulate the inner workings of the psyche is a process in the pursuit of the Self: of Individuation, the Philosopher's Stone, and the Grail, to unlock doors.

The Animus, the Anima, and the archetypal Seeker working in concert clarify the problem, negotiate a solution, and together finally pull the door open giving the group potential access to the Castle. The hero has been tested and the treasure is his quest. In another version it could be the Goddesses that would have bestowed the gifts on the hero to conquer the monsters, outwit the giants and the other creatures that inhabit the mythical realm.

What is the treasure? The treasure is that which we seek. What has been sought after since man begins to think about himself, his world, his existence, the cosmos, and life itself. That search is what we share with our ancestors. The search for balance, harmony, peace, the Self, Individuation, Heaven, and Nirvana, all which alchemists refer to as the Philosopher's Stone. The search is what it means to be a human being, the good, the bad, and the wonder of life. And the search is what this writing is about. That is why mythology, and the ancient writings are important. These and all the other treasured resources are breadcrumbs that lead us out of the forest into the light.

Note above that the treasure has not been found nor the castle reached. It may be a treasure that can never be found. Maybe it does not exist. But if there is to be a future for the planet, the search must go on.

There are more breadcrumbs in this vision than even I am seeing. It is a mythical-magical experience. The three journeyers set out on the path and walk side by side rather than trailing in a row, which is the usual formation. Animus and Anima are in balance, and with intuition, wisdom, and logic an obstacle was overcome, and the castle with its fluttering pennants beckoning from the misty distance can be seen.

Chapter 15

Calcinatio

The alchemical process of *Calcinatio* is the psychological operation that has to do with fire in its many manifestations, which is experienced on the path of those seeking Individuation. Since early history *Calcinatio* was noted to be the catalyst for transformation from one state of being to another. The unknown property of fire being mysterious and powerful loaned itself well to the realm of magic. Its transformative powers did not go unnoticed and became a mainstay of everyday life. That it became embedded in the psyche early in our history is understandable and is the most easily recognized of the alchemical operations for the practitioner. An abbreviated account follows provided by a client journeyer dealing with incest issues. I will refer to her as Lydia in this and following passages.

Lydia, 30 years old, single, bright, and successful in her career chose to try Journeying after successive and prolonged various therapies and interventions to help resolve childhood abuse issues. These issues interfered with her ability to sustain relationships and affected her self-image in negative ways that led to depression and withdrawal. During her initial Journey and after acquiring allies, she was eager to confront her primary issues of abuse.

Lydia: Journey One

I felt very strong and safe at this time, surrounded by all my allies and their medicine, and asked my father to join us. He did. He looked as he did right before he died of emphysema, very sick and frail. I asked him why he did what he did to me. He didn't answer immediately, and I felt great rage. The mountain lion struck at him with her right paw and tore his head off. His body crumpled to the ground. Seeing him so injured made me feel compassion. I asked the mountain lion to heal him. She waved her paw over him, and he was whole. He youthened until he was a small boy. He laid on the ground, crying. I felt compassion for him as a vulnerable little boy, and because of whatever happened to him to make him the way he was.

One of Lydia's demons is rage. This rage is psychic energy she has carried for many years. I refer to these energies as demons in that they interfere with our lives in ways that are detrimental to our happiness and well-being. And they are real. If they did not constitute a reality, they would not have an effect on us. The Shaman recognizes these demons and knows how to vanquish them. The battle may be bloody and gruesome but necessary.

Lydia's encounter with her father provided her the opportunity to engage that demon. But her resistance to being able to fight him or inflict a gruesome punishment on him, or anyone, prevented her from effectively engaging her demon. Interestingly, she manifested another demon, a lesser one, the guilt she felt for punishing her father. Her error was to resurrect him. Her shadow is active in several ways here, first the repression of rage, then the repression of wanting to punish her father.

Demons are a component of our spiritual makeup. Included are rage, fear, shame, insecurities of all kinds, and everything that hinders or blocks growth and happiness. Everything we do, feel, experience is filtered through that matrix. It is like a television receiver with a faulty component. The incoming signal may be pure and strong, but that component may result in a distorted image. One's power is diminished by so many in so many ways. From childhood on someone is chipping away at our powerbase until one is afraid, reluctant to spread their wings and fly, leap from the cliff's edge into the expanse laid out before them.

The other aspect of the psychic spectrum is the upper world component. Just as therein reside the scurrilous demons, the upper world of the psychic phenomena (super ego), is inhabited by superheroes, allies of all breeds and manner. The array of allies is limited only by the imagination of the journeyer. Each situation calls for a particular response. Every individual has preconceived ideas as to what their allies should be, but those desires seldom manifest in that way. If one is facing a menacing entity, one would expect an ally of tremendous strength, but instead a mouse may manifest and somehow defeat or trick this demon. And the journeyer will understand and appreciate that entity. One cannot acquire allies from a list in a book or by preference. They are acquired by engaging the adventure, through accepting the challenge, and embarking on the journey. Magicians, fairies, wise men or women, animals of every ilk, entities of energy, plants, stones, relatives who have passed, mythical figures, and anything one can imagine are possible. These psychic entities are as real as are the demons in this world where few dare to enter. Lydia vented her rage against her father, something she had carried for most of her life. But she also made a critical error.

Shamans, for millennia, have understood that events occur within the psychic realm, the spirit world. Eventually they are housed deep in the lower world, and remain as spiritual matter, psychic energy. To engage that matter, one must journey to where it lives, pacing, looking for a chink in the armor to escape its gatekeepers. The journey is real, as real as any other experience in any other realm. And therein lies the effectiveness of the hard-won battles and confrontations with these demons. Should one face, battle and conquer a demon in this world of the Shaman, it has the same effect as if it had occurred in the middle world.

The Shadow Knows

During the 1940s, the radio era, a popular show began in the following way: "Who knows what evil lurks in the hearts of men? The Shadow knows!" Its popularity drew on the fascination with the dark side of who we are, that part of our humanity that is repressed. It is the part that says, "Oh, I could never do that. How could they do that awful thing to another human being?" Yet if those people who have those reactions had been born in a different place under different circumstances, they could very well behave in the manner that they are resisting. Hitler personified the shadow of an entire nation and brought it into the light for the world to see. Many individuals describe Hitler as an unfathomable monster. But we all share the same propensity for every evil ever committed and the capacity for the greatest self-sacrifice and goodness.

It is important to recognize that the shadow is not only evil. The shadow is anything that is repressed, the unexpressed love of a man for another man, the desire to be a dancer rather than a policeman. The deepest desires and unexpressed wishes are relegated to the shadow lingering there like bats clinging to the roof of a darkened cave.

The job of the Shaman is to guide and advise the journeyer in their process. Lydia was instructed that if she encounters a demon and feels threatened, she should destroy it. She should unleash the full force of her strength to reclaim her power.

This power belongs to the journeyer, in this case Lydia. One does not ask for it but takes it by whatever means necessary. She was instructed to descend to the lower world and engage that demon once again with further instructions as to how to proceed. This is to be done without remorse, without regret. If there are remains, the warrior is to bury them, throw them into water, or incinerate those remains in fire. Here is alchemy at work per Lydia: *Calcinatio*.

Lydia: Journey Two

As I prepare to enter, I call for dog. She is waiting for me and leads me down. When we emerge into the lower world, dog leaves me. I am in the valley surrounded by mountains again. I meet a rattlesnake who asks me to let him bite my finger. I agree. As his venom flows into me I become very warm and feel great power surge through me. I feel very strong, invincible.

I decide now I will deal with my father. I call for my allies and they appear, bear, mountain lion, wolf, tree. Then I call for my father. He appears and I ask him why he raped me. He said to control and dominate me. I asked him why he wanted to hurt me. He said because he wanted me to know the pain he had known as a child.

I feel my rage grow and I let it out. He is covered with rattlesnakes. They slither over him, biting him, scaring him. Several snakes wrap themselves around me, but they are my friends. They do not harm me. I ask him how it feels to be so terrified, unable to move or escape. As the snakes bite him, I ask him how it feels to know pain. Mountain lion approaches him and slowly rakes her claws down his chest, not killing but causing great pain.

He collapses from fear. A spear appears in my hand. I plunge it into his heart and twist it, killing him. My allies all voice my victory by howling-roaring. I drag him by the hair to a nearby river. He starts to float away. I stop it because I do not want him to resurface later. Beaver appears and drags him down to the river's bed. Beaver shoves him through the earth's crust. I send him to the molten center of the earth, and he explodes into flames, thoroughly incinerated.

Her shadow is evident at this point. One does not torture and kill one's father. That desire must be carried to the grave unless that energy can be effectively discharged in a journey, as Lydia demonstrated. She uses Alchemy here without knowledge of that process. When father is thrust into the molten earth, that energy is transformed via the alchemical process of *Calcinatio*.

Alchemy is supposedly a lost art but is frequently the catalyst for transformation in the Shaman's world. Lydia utilizes fire to transform her rage. C. G. Jung refers to this particular process as the alchemical stage of *Calcinatio*, and the elements are of fire and heat. The associated images are of erotic love as well as the emotions of primitive anger, frustration, and rage which are initiated in the love relationship. *Calcinatio* represents being burned up, consumed by these unmet desires, frustrations, passions, and rage. And the transformative power of fire to cleanse, purify, and alter are well known in the shamanic alchemical process.

How does the adventurer decide which issues to engage? The answer is simple. One doesn't. Whatever has the most emotional weight will rise to the front of the line. In Lydia's case it was the abuse issue, and she went straight to that arena. In her initial encounter with her father, she did confront him but had not been infused with the power she needed to effectively follow through to a resolution. She had courage though. After the encounter with Rattlesnake, Lydia then was able to unleash the full potential of her power. Rattlesnake is one of her power allies. In typical shamanic fashion, Rattlesnake's venom is transformed into power. She states, "They give me their venom, I give them my blood."

Lydia: Journey Two (Cont'd)

I feel victorious and celebrate by dancing around a fire with my spear. I wish to thank Rattlesnake in a special way for his help. I cut my left wrist with a knife and feed Rattlesnake my blood. Many snakes cover the land. A mother snake shows me her clutch of eggs which hatch as we watch. The mother snake asks me to allow her children to bite my fingers. I do so. They give me their venom; I give them my blood.

A familiar man appears, and we embrace. Rattlesnakes cover us, binding us together. We make love and he disappears. I feel the need to cleanse and purify. I wish to immerse myself in water but refuse the river as it has been contaminated by my father. Instead I bathe in a small pond. A mother turtle and her babies are watching when I surface. The pond is their home and I thank them for allowing me to use it.

When I emerge from the pond, I spend time wondering what it would be like to be a snake. I transform into a snake (shapeshifting). I feel very warm and powerful although I know those who touch me may find my skin cold. I crawl into my burrow. A mouse enters and I eat him, very tasty. Rabbit enters and I swallow her, but it is difficult because she is so big. I am told I am swallowing my own fear and transmuting it into courage.

I emerge from my burrow and a bald eagle gently, but firmly grasps me in his talons. We fly over a great distance. For the first time in years, I am not afraid of flying, I'm enjoying it. I can see for miles in the air. Eagle flies me to the Southwest where I see my ally Agape howling on a mesa. We fly down into South America to the Amazon. Eagle leaves me on a riverbank and circles overhead, watching.

A huge snake, three or four stories high, rises

from the river. He is black with a yellow throat and belly. He tells me he is Skaa. I ask him why I was brought before him. He tells me I need to realize I have been given great courage and power. I ask what he has to tell me. He says I am to reveal my pain in my writing so that others may be healed. I thank Skaa for his words of encouragement. Eagle picks me and very rapidly flies me back to the valley. I become human again.

Next *Cuniunctio*, (union of opposites that have been imperfectly separated) in the encounter with a man, then *Solutio* in a cleansing pond. The alchemical operations are demonstrated in various presentations. It is important to recognize these in their many facets.

Lydia celebrates and dances. Dance is performed in preparation for or celebration of. Fire is the Sacred Self. Lydia also enters a cleansing process involving water, another Jungian alchemical process, *Solutio*. The themes of opposites, fire and water, persist. She has acquired a weapon, the spear, which will come to light again in future journeys.

It is common for more than one alchemical and shamanic processes to occur during the journey. Lydia glosses over an important event when she writes about her encounter with a man with whom she makes love. This is an important event in that it is the incorporation of the masculine aspect of herself and a movement to wholeness, *Coniunctio* or the union of opposites. Everyone is familiar with the Taoist Yin-Yang symbol, wherein each half contains the seed of its opposite and comprises the whole. Its endurance as a symbol reflects a profound truth in a beautiful balanced image. It is the primordial energy that gives birth to the manifest world and ten thousand things.

The content of this journey is inspirational in its expansiveness. Lydia shapeshifts to Snake and savors the experience of the power of snake. She devours a mouse and rabbit and understands the reality of transmuting her fear into courage. Her rage is transformed by the alchemical operation of fire and water into power in the form of the snake, Skaa.

And if that is not enough, her fear of flying is vanquished. On return from the journey, when she ascends to the middle world she writes, "I become human again." It is a profound statement of the healing nature of her journey.

Chapter 16

Solutio

Solutio is one of the major operations in the alchemical operations and pertains to liquids. In this operation a solid is transformed through liquid. It also signifies the return of differentiated matter to its undifferentiated state or original state, *Prima Materia*. In various creation myths, the world and everything in it originated from water as primary material. Flood stories of epic proportions appear in many cultures and are presented as cleansing transformative events.

In transformative shamanic encounters, the initiate must first "go to their bones" to be broken down to their undifferentiated state to be reconstructed. The myth of Inanna details her descent into the lower world, during which she is stripped of all her worldly possessions, even her flesh, and then hung on a hook. She is eventually rescued and ascends fully formed to take her rightful place in the heavens. The following is a dream I had which highlights both the operation of *Solutio* and the concept of *Prima Materia*.

Author's Dream of 1996

I am working in an institution for men, a security

unit. As I walk down a hall, I see a young man hiding in a doorway and using a phone. I know he should not be there, and I summon help because I know the young man will probably fight. Help arrives and the young man is subdued. He is taken to a room where there is a steel drum with a thick-dark liquid in it. A man puts a pill in the liquid and stirs it.

The young man is thrust into the drum and thrashes about for a short while and then apparently disappears and can no longer be seen. No one seems to be concerned.

The issue underlying this action is the concern for the loss of youth. Through the operation of *Solutio* the "young man" is returned to *Prima Materia*, the dark liquid, and the next phase of Individuation can commence. This next phase could not begin until the young man is transformed by the processes which follow further on in this text. Even though the young man fights this movement, in the end the general lack of concern suggests the operation was correct and proper.

The dream is quite rich in a Jungian sense in that much of the symbolism found is the repetition of the previous account. Here we encounter a vivid concept of *Prima Materia*. The chaos and raw material that when subjected to a series of operations results in the Philosophers Stone, Individuation.

Chapter 17

Buried Alive

In the year 2000, I was buried alive in an initiatory ceremony. In a grave, dug by me, six feet deep, six feet long, I was to spend the night there from sunset to sunrise. The purpose of the ceremony was a ritual death and rebirth process, a vision quest.

Prior to this event, a period of preparation took place where I engaged in a Journey with a fellow Shaman, and spent time in a purification process in a hot springs cave. Once the purification process was complete, I fasted for three days, and then entered a period of silence and meditation. It should be stressed that this process should only be undertaken under the supervision of a qualified Shaman.

Next, I was to dig my own grave. The process of digging the grave is an important procedure. It puts one in touch with the inevitable and gives one time to meditate on that finality. Even though death and burial is a universal event, it is probably the most ignored process in our culture. Every effort and expense are directed at prolonging life even in the most critical cases. Most individuals who undergo the shamanic journey process will address that issue and will come to terms with death in a way that is seen as a natural event, not to be feared or prolonged but to be accepted as a natural transition. It is a simple contract signed at birth between the sacred and the profane. One will be born, live and die, no promises, no directives, just the wonderful gift of life.

On the day of my internment, guests and relatives arrived, as if responding to a funeral notice they had received, to find my person laid out in my journey space in my best suit and presumably dead. Masked, I lay in state, and one by one the guests would enter, sit or stand at my side, and say the things one says during those times. Farewells, confessions, grievances, appreciations, and declarations of love spilled out into the still quietness of the occasion to be taken to my grave where I would be given my final resting place.

If it appears there is a considerable amount of space dedicated to the subject of death, it is because the reality of death has a major impact on our lives and is of paramount importance. All roads wend their way to that inescapable finality. Plans and dreams about how we want to live, in the end, give way to thoughts about the end of the Journey. How we react to thoughts about our inevitable end, death, influences how we live our lives.

In the shamanic intervention there is an important concept of transformation. This is brought about by the ceremonies that require death and finally rebirth through a series of alchemical processes. As one traverses these pages one begins to see the patterns and scripts that are played out time and time again.

Nigredo, Putrefactio, Albedo, Mortificatio

We begin to see the drama played out in this experience of an initiatory burial, wherein the various alchemical operations can be discerned. The body of this event is taken from my experience in the grave. It is presented in a narrative style that mimics the concomitant altered state of consciousness. Hence, one will note a dramatic difference in the following writing from the previous chapters. This is an attempt to replicate that experience.

Smoke and Mirrors

Having slipped into a dreamworld, *un sueno*, I find myself unable to awaken from it, and now I seek escape from that which I had wished for. *Ay, Madre mia.* Not escape as in deceased and being lowered with solemnity into an obscure and dampened pit. But rather a return to reality as I knew it before the slip, where everything stood telephone-pole orderly, where event and causation danced to the rhythm of reason. Although the slip may not have been a slip at all. It may have been more of a gradual deconstruction-restructuring process that occurred as I passed unconcerned through an event horizon. To find my way home though, it may be of some value to know how my reality shifted. That is the reason I talk of this, that and no other. Ah, you laugh, but remember this. *Por la risa se saca el tonto.* A fool is known by his laughing. Draw near, for I can only speak of this in hushed breaths. And still, know that I feel no malice toward those who mock my tale. I understand. You see *estuve enterado vivo.* I was buried alive. *Por Dios. Si, es la verdad.*

Examining that event, that fool-headed burial, returns me to my fevered mental meanderings as perhaps being crucial to understanding how and when the slip occurred. Had I laid maiden-plaited threads behind me, like Theseus into the maze, my escape would have been assured. I didn't because I knew not what I had ventured into. And I only speak of the event now because not to will surely banish all hope of my much sought after resurrection. Yet is hope not truly the great horned deceiver? And since when have the hopes of mankind ever been realized?

Yes. It was a dare, bravado laden, so casually tossed out I didn't see it for what it truly held. They, friends— Ha! More like tormentors—taunted me to lie in a fresh dug and darkened grave. *De broma? A joke?* I dismissed my trepidations much too quickly. Now they seem a lighthouse beacon piercing a storm-tossed darkness that should have turned my bow to port. So, why did I go into that cursed hole? Perhaps it is this that I must answer, this that I must confess. And if it is the right confession, I believe I shall then be liberated from this hellish existence.

That you are a stranger is no accident as this is a difficult revelation. I could not bare my soul to just anyone that I would later have to see across a room. They pretending they do not know my abominable secret, and I knowing they do. *Cada uno sabe donde le aprieta el zapato.* Each one knows where his own shoe pinches.

Though it is difficult to admit, it's best I say it outright. You see. *Soy cobarde.* Oy, my tongue, still it seeks to guard my secrets. I am a coward! *Sí.* There, it has been spoken. And yes, I took the coward's way out. The alternative was to decline the taunt and show my cowardice to all. At least in my sodden sanctuary, there beneath the cover of darkness, no one would see my insecurities, my fears of death. Or is it Life that I fear? I don't know and don't think I want to know. I trembled at the thought of worms, red and fleshy like fat fingers, crawling about me. Measuring me. For what reason? To determine if I truly did measure up? *Gusanos. Madre Mia.*

So armored in my fear, I took up the gauntlet. "Act in haste, repent in leisure" was most assuredly born of this act. If I speak of that fateful decision with what may, to some, seem like conviction, know that it is more the utterances of madness conceived by the existence of a shadow cast by an unseen truth, the shadow provides only reference to the true nature of its origin. With that in mind, my friend, and with your indulgence, I will continue my narrative in diminishing hope of resurrection from this shade-populated existence.

That you would appear to be concerned is an indulgence, but that you were chosen to hear this accounting, now that is an honor. You see, there is the element of confession here, and the one to whom the confession is being made is afforded a position of authority. For is it not through the portiere of the confessional that the gates of heaven are broached? Perhaps it was that very angelic beckoning from those celestial heights that enticed me, even as it does now. Why else a confessor? Even *los sin verguenza*, the shameless, seek an ear turned to their secret maleficence. *Verdad?*

A priest?

No! No. Yo creo que no. That's not what I want.

A ritual? No, gracias.

What I seek are guideposts that I might follow back to the place where I slipped into this reverie. Now I merely exist as a dream dreamed by a great dreamer and fear that when that dreamer awakens so goes the dreamed. Do we all not want to occupy the abode of the dreamer, he who orchestrates the fugue?

Oh yes. I am riddled with fears, *tengo mucho miedo, mucho.* Yes. Fears, great and small and perhaps I will speak of them if you deem it necessary, even though I am loath to examine certain truths about myself. Certainly, you can understand my reticence. *Verdad? Tengo miedo que estoy perdido en perdicion. Ay, Perdon a mi, Senor.* Surely there must be some unrevealed facet of yourself you wish to keep from public scrutiny. *Que no?*

Ha! But please don't fret that behind my desire to confess is a hunger to unburden a fitful conscience. It is so much more beastly. It was to my own desires and pleasures that I reached for prior to the slip, and it is to that which I now still aspire. Do you not have a sense of my desperation, my friend? But please don't judge me too harshly there. My sin is but a venial sin, one of pride I suspect, a couple of Our Fathers in penance, *mi creo.*

Because in that same desperation to not be revealed for what I truly am, yes, you may speak it, a coward, I accepted the challenge of tomb sleeping.

Entendes? So desperate was I that I even agreed to dig my own grave. *Un tumba sepulcro.* Shovel by shovel I excavated and as the blisters formed, then broke finally weeping my body fluids into the earth, I recognized in each shovel full of dirt taken from the grave my passing days. One shovel of dirt, one day lived. Both activities leading to the same inevitable destination, finality, and an observation. One will find, my friend, that the proportion of earth taken from the grave is greater than the grave's capacity to contain it. Pero of what value is that revelation to me, or anyone? *Que no?*

Yet I attended to that distasteful task dutifully and gave thanks that the ground was not hard and that there were no stones. Crows and magpies danced in the treetops swaying with the heated breeze, knowing full well, at least I thought, the purpose of my beguiled activity. Certainly, better than I, since I had not ever been a man of introspection. No, I saw no redemption in that practice. Had I known that hole to be what it was though, a gateway, a portal, *si, perdicion*, I would have filled it with stone and dirt and planted it over to conceal all traces of it. And should I do that now, it might seal off my return. Maybe in recreating my death, *mi muerte*, I will be reborn. Or what if I still rest in that place and only dreamed my climb out of that pit?

I recall or believe that I recall, that after an interminable passage of time buried there, I awoke and found myself again in darkness. I panicked and flailed my arms about knocking dirt into my face until I remembered where I had lain. Santa Maria.

Try as I might I could not contain my fear. I leapt to my feet and struggled against my roof. Ignoring the splinters, I pushed with all my strength and felt the weight of the earth above me and then it began to give way. Again the dirt into my face and mouth and then a new sun on my new face, *si, el sol,* and I forgot about the dirt. The sun so beautiful, the sky too much an extension of my person, I felt I could reach up and capture a bit in my hands. Now I question whether this actually occurred. Perhaps I dreamed that escape while I lay deep in my tomb. It seems mythical in its proportion. Can you possibly comprehend my consternation, neighbor?

Forgive me this intrusion, my friend. I cannot compensate your kindness, but surely you will be rewarded in heavenly merit. If you name me mad, I will accept that gladly and call it done for it is reason that I seek. And madness would be reason. But first hear me out.

When first I climbed down into my grave and lay with my arms crossed, I played the role of *los sin vida* quite well, I thought. But then I'd already had plenty of practice except it was above ground, and I had walked around in it. Words I don't recall were pronounced and friends and *mi familia* peered down at me and some dropped flowers. *Valgame Dios,* it was lovely. I heard a woman weep, *mi esposa, llorando* tears of quiet loss and the nervous laughter of the unsure and the unsettled.

Ah, the evening, *si,* that dark evening. This affair took place in dismal rain and lightning that washed the scene in white light that made ghosts of those gathered there. The guests shielded themselves as best they could against the elements with dark umbrellas that hovered like silent bats above their heads. That weather certainly provided me an excuse to back out of that ludicrous bargain. Yet I persisted, *como un perro* worrying a bone. Oh, how many times, now, I wished I had taken that opportunity. There is one other thing that comes to my mind, though. Let me tell you about *los gusanos*. The ground crawled with worms, squirming wet worms. *Gusanos* everywhere. Never had I seen so many, so many a person could not take a step without crushing the wriggling forms with each feeble footfall. So many signs, so many, *como un tonto*, I ignored.

Yet, I suppose, that if this is to be a righteous confession, I will admit I did feel favored. After all, was I not the pivotal player in this highest of dramas? *Si. Quise ser un perla*, be a jewel, for them to weep for me, dash their body upon my casket, tear their hair, rent their clothing. After all, was I not entitled to at least that? *Yo creo que si.*

Then planks were placed over the opening until only thin slices of evening light cut the darkness gathering about me. I did not know the extent of my friends, mis amigos, intent for my initiation, if that is what it was. It may have been a schoolboy prank borne by the sheer momentum of it all, but why worry that now? Shovels full of dirt fell with finality atop the planks and at first some filtered through, and I closed my eyes against the dying light. When the dirt quit falling and I opened my eyes, I found my world gone. There was no sound, no ray of light, no horizon to keep one anchored to the ground. Nothing existed. *Estuvo en oscurro puro*, and the earth was a formless void and darkness covered the face of the deep. Mockery? *No. No. Valgame no*. It was at that moment that I knew my death.

Mi primero piensamiente, my first thought, *antes del horror*, caused my person to tremble, *bone deep, si a mis huesos*. I understood that no matter how great or insignificant one has been, saint or sinner, we will all find ourselves in the end at this worm's banquet. So why strive? Why worry? *No se*.

O, la terror? Por Dios. Quiria gritar. Como dice? Shriek. *Si, scream. Si. Pero no puediera*. I could not. My breath it would not come. It held fast in my throat *como hielo*, like ice. *Y mi corazon*, whew, I knew it would burst from my breast. And I pleaded *con El Senor, Ayudame!* Help me!

The air, it did not stir. It too was dead. It lay like a tombstone, heavy and hard upon me till I too could not stir. It pressed the life from my wretched body and all I could do was shrink against the embracing bosom of our welcoming mother, the earth.

Then, it, *si, la muerte*, lay peaceful and light against me, a languid lover. How long I lay there I do not know. Hours, days, months, eons. *No se*.

My flesh began to slough from my bones. First the pallid skin like parchment pages torn from the holy books of time, then my writhing muscles and snaking tendons until finally my heart fell tumbling from my chest and lay beating, unknowing on the damp ground, pulsing the remnants of rusted blood. It pooled and steamed there momentarily then seeped into the dark below. And the worms? *Los gusanos?* Oh yes. They were there, fat and wriggling and plentiful. Initially, the revulsion seized my courage and dashed it upon the rocks of reason until it lay shredded like forgotten wreckage. But they set about their task with such diligence anyway. They consumed the dead and putrid flesh from my body and picked my bones clean and white and polished. At last, I lay in my bones, my porcelain perfect bones, and I in return appreciated their thoroughness and their efficiency and thanked them for their services. I had been purified, made virtuous.

    Long I lingered, perhaps I slumbered when a voice fell upon me. A voice of music, melodious, and it drew me up into the star-scattered vacuum of space. And there before a scarlet moon that pulsed like a great heart organ of the night, she revealed herself to me. *Una diosa.*

    Mists and vapors gathered, swirled, and took form. Oh, not solid form. There were misty places and more solid forms so that I could see stars beyond her at once here and see the texture of her fine pale skin there. And I felt drawn, an addict to his seductress. She held out her arms to me, and I went to her. She folded me to her breast, and I wanted to remain there forever. I felt the urge to suckle there. I sought her breast among her tattered drapes fumbling like a youthful lover. Perhaps I offended because with considerable force she shoved me to the ground where I lay in my consternation. What crime had I committed? The crime of desire? *Quien sabe?*

Then in a soft, sweet voice that beguiled, she spoke. No, it seemed more a song. I am not your mother. Nor am I your lover. But still, she held out her arms to me. And I, even in my confusion, longed for the warmth of her ethereal embrace. Oh to be able to once again, just for a moment, one earthly moment, lie in the light of her arms. *Ay, Dios Mio.*

Who are you? I cried out to her. I know you. I am certain of that. Reveal yourself that I might dismiss my doubts.

Bones: From the Cave Gallery sculpture collection.
"The worms picked my bones clean."

No, she answered me back in that voice of heavenly song. You know of me. But you do not know me.

Hah! You're not even real. You're just a wisp of smoke and some mirrors, I told her. Yeah, I told her straight up. You know what she did? She leaned over, looked me dead in the eye and spat in that very eye. *Si. Es la verdad. La verdad.*

Upset? No, I will confess to something stronger: anger. I came to my feet, raised a fist to her and spoke to her in most unflattering terms. *Quise darla una soberana palizo.* I wanted to give her a good trouncing.

But she only smiled at me and spoke softly. If I am only smoke, why clutch at that which you cannot grasp?

Look at you, I shouted after her, your gowns are rags and your staff nothing but a twisted branch of a dead tree. *Un palo.*

Ah, yes, she told me and thrashed me about the head with that cursed stick, knocking me again to the ground. And you are responsible for my rags and poor staff. Manifestations are not what they used to be. Decline in demand, you see. I do long so for the celestial presentation. There was a time I would be heralded by a thousand golden trumpets, accompanied by a hundred lutes and a hundred harps wrought of the finest of woods. Cherubim and seraphim would scatter dew-dropped flower petals before my feet. And the lighting, first class all the way, golden hues fading in and out. Scents of Frankincense and Myrrh wafting on warm and gentle breezes prevailed. Yes, I do long for the days of David.

I admit I was smitten by her. *Senti amor por ella. Si. De veras.* She was so much more than a wisp of ethereal beauty. She embodied the entire history of women, the beguiler, the seductress, *madre*, lover, saint, whore, wife and *diosa*, all beneath a mane of smoke grey hair that floated about a delicately chiseled yet skeletal continence. *Si, cuero y huesos.* Skin and bones. I could see that her ragged shroud was once a fine silken vestment, now a faded purple. *Vestido de reina.* A queen. Tarnished gold trim spoke of greater glory. Yet she still held high authority and continued to regale me with her nonsense. Well then, I pleaded, *con todo mi corizon,* are you here to grant me absolution? I knew it to be a pitiful plea yet felt compelled to take the chance that perhaps she bore the kings signet and could grant me my boon.

She pointed a long pale finger at me *que era como un hueso blanco,* a white bone and spoke in such a soft tone I strained my ear to hear what she said. In the end, she whispered, the Greeks said it best. There is really no witness so terrible, no accuser so powerful as the conscience that dwells within our breast.

Are you saying I can free myself from this hell? That's all I really wanted from her, some hope, some magical intonation that would transport me back to that time and place where I had lived a normal existence. *Ahora no soy ni la sombra mi mismo.* Am I not even the shadow of my former self?

Then she spoke again, and I felt my blood

begin to boil. The mind of its own self can make a heaven of hell or a hell of heaven. She took on a saintly composure, all light and forbearance.

I suppose it provoked me so that I lost patience and raised my voice against her. Clichés, I shouted after her. That's all you have to offer!

That's all there is, she addressed me as if to a child. *Si, como un niño.* There is nothing new under the sun. Life is cliche.

Enough! Let me be, Mistress, I hurled back at her. I ask for wisdom, and you provide dusty words.

Life is but a walking shadow, I heard her say, and her voice became increasingly faint. A poor player that . . .

And that's all I could make out. Now what the hell does that have to do with anything, with my conundrum? And then she began to decay until there was only I standing alone, *solamente*, shaking an impotent fist at the gathering stars beyond.

Again, I beg forbearance, friend, and if I am impertinent to infer friendship it is because you have indulged the odious ravings of one such as I. *Pero entiendes que no soy loco.*

Con su permiso, mi amigo. May I lay my hand upon your shoulder so that I might know if you are indeed corporeal? Perhaps I should explain.

Why did I not simply climb out of that gruesome pit? Well, to my discredit, I did just that. Or perhaps I didn't. You see I had vowed to myself that I would endure this ordeal and prove that, especially to myself, yes, I did have courage. The darkest hour came upon me and unable to endure the crucible beyond that point I struck the mantle above me that held me a consenting prisoner and scrambled out into the cool starlit night. Free. And on searching for justification to abandon my covenant I did not have to seek beyond the most mundane of rationales when I found I could not endure my trial. But defer judgement, *por favor*, until you have heard me out. *Gracias*.

And so, like the shipmates of Odysseus. I succumbed to the voice of the Sirens that lay just beyond my internment, comfort, and warmth. Folly, I proclaimed. This is but a charade contrived by others, and I no longer wish to engage in this madness.

Relieved and confident in my actions I entered the blessed warmth of the dimly lit house. There were candles still burning, some sputtering their final light on the alter near where I had lain in state so long ago. A peaceful quiet warmed me some. The light of a dim lamp guided me to a bedroom, but on entering, I found that the guests that had stayed over now slumbered there. In an adjacent room the scene was repeated but in the third I found an empty bed and quickly without removing my clothing lay beneath the warmth of a down comforter. Never before had I appreciated more the exquisite comfort of the bed and the warmth of the covering. Ah such a blessing.

Then, my friend, I sensed a prickle of uneasiness, *como puedo decir*, how can I say, like a mist had settled on me. My comfort abated and I realized with much dismay that the bed I lay in was not my bed, that this was not even my home and that in fact I still lay in the impenetrable darkness and cold of my tomb. I am loathing to admit this, but I wept like a child. *Si, como un nino. Y por eso*, that is why I want to touch your shoulder. How else am I to know if you are but a vapor or not?

All I ask is to find my way home, strong winds at my back to fill my sails, stars to guide my sight and to be restored to my place in the world that I knew. *Nada mas*.

Still, be you vapor, mist or phantom, grant me absolution that I might find peace in my delirium. If that is not your jurisdiction, indicate by word or gesture, and I will take my leave so as not to impinge on your gracious forbearance.

Entiendes, mi amigo, that I am cognizant of the character of my presentation, that I grasp at smoke. *Si, yo se. Pero que puedo hacer?*

Ah. Si, entiendo. Yes, I understand. Men through the ages have sought to attain, to grasp on to that which is mercurial. *Si. Tambien yo.* Yes, I do comprehend. *Con su permisio, un momento, mi amigo*, that I might ponder your words as they do have the ring of veracity. The clarity cuts through the addled fog of my confusion like a newly forged and tempered steel rapier. It may be the key though, a map to guide me out of this wallowing greyness.

You say I am alive, *verdad?* Walking among the living? *Que soy vivo? Creie que estuvo muerto.* That I was dead and in a place inhabited by those crossed over the river, that inexorable river that has flowed to a yellow-mirrored sea even at the night of time. Yet, see how tenaciously the flesh does cling to its determined form.

Por Dios. Es la verdad. I did want to live forever, feared death, and knew the terror of the king's stag being pursued, wide-eyed, by hell-born hounds in the shadowed forest. But now as I speak, I sense an illumination smoldering in those misted woods.

Yes. Yes, I remember now. Ah yes. As I lay buried in my lone and unconsecrated grave, a vision mercifully disturbed my cold solitude. I at first gave thanks for this interlude even if it beheld the lunacy of an already questionably moldering mind.

In this dream within a dream, I found myself at a gathering of a multitude of tradesmen. Four entertainers performed at their craft in a great hall upon a stage. Their diversion consisted of heckling those in attendance. One produced an air rifle and proceeded to pelt the gathering. When they focused on me, I ran from the room with them in pursuit, laughing. Quickly, I put distance between us and considered them clowns, *piasos, tontos. Que podria piensar?* What could I think?

Then just as I sensed relief to be shed of them, they reappeared, this time *con pistolas* and an automatic rifle. Can you imagine? *Si. Verdad.* My annoyance turned to frightened alarm. *Entiendes?* Again I struck out, this time into a wooded area. I ran until my heart pounding, my breath burning in my lungs I could go no further. My legs would not hold me up.

At a sweeping turn on a rutted and muddy

trail, there they confronted me. With their weapons trained on me, as if I could run any farther, I was prodded on to a ramshackle house and locked in an empty room. *Por que?* They would not speak to me or tell me why they comported themselves in this abominable manner. *Pero, mi tenia miedo por mi vida. Si,* I feared for my very life. I knew their unspoken intention but could not fathom reason beyond sadistic pleasures.

Pero escape de la casa. You see they did not realize that I had been confined in a room with an entrance to the outside. I rejoiced, seized on the opportunity, changed my clothing for camouflaged wear I appropriated from a closet and made my bid for freedom and safety.

I chose a route down a steep incline and fled deep into the woods. There I secreted my person in a clump of scrub oak and feeling invisible and secure in my haven, I rested. *Paz. Senti la paz.* Blessed Peace.

Having eluded my murderous pursuers, *gracias a Dios,* I reveled in the relief. *Si. Que delicia.* But then even as the calmness settled into me, I heard a dreadful sound, a four-wheel vehicle, its engine whining, making its way down the steep slope and directly toward me. How was that possible, friend? *No se.* I do not know.

At the same time, a voice, familiar and hard *como una piedra,* like a stone striking me on the chest hurled me into a black, black fear, into Tartarus, that place of darkest gloom in the underworld, a dark so dense, inescapable, it pressed upon my eyes, my ears, my very soul. *Mi animas.*

Because, from out of the purpled dusk one of the hunters appeared before me, dark and foreboding and with his *pistola* commanded me from my concealment, impossible though it was to discover, I had believed. And then, he did something odd. First, he flagged his *compadres*, then he tossed his *pistola* at my feet and nodded for me to take it up. Just a slow deliberate gesture that somehow assured me. My fear? It lessened. Still, I could see the others approaching in the fading light of the forest.

He nodded once again, and I finally understood. This was salvation. Finally, an ally. I stooped to retrieve the *pistola* with much relief and a sense of overwhelming gratitude for this friend. Tears of joy came to my eyes, and he offered up a gracious face of compassion and my heart sang.

Over the crest of a rise, in an earth-tearing rush, the others bore down on us in their merciless machine. The *pistola*, heavy and cold steel, solid, pressed gratefully into my quivering sweat-drenched grip, and with my newfound *compadre* at my side I felt a determined belief that, yes, I would forestall my hatefully designed demise. My advantage lay in the element of surprise. I could not speak for the dryness of my mouth and the hot breath that tore at my throat, or I would have extended my enduring indebtedness to my comrade for fostering renewed hope in my hour of deprivation.

Bushes and small aspens fell snapping and whipping before their mechanized advance on our position. As they neared, I positioned myself near a stout pine tree to use as a shield and barrier, and from where I could make a gun-blazing stand. They would not take me without spilling blood of their own. Perhaps they would even abandon their crazed sport when they realized I had the means to protect myself.

My benefactor slipped into the shadows and the others happened upon me in an instant. I feared my pounding heart would reveal my presence, but a revived reassurance lifted my spirits and rekindled my courage. The *pistola*, one I was familiar with, would change the direction of this harrowing encounter. I released the safety, and chambered a round. I panicked. Something was wrong with the sound of the action. And in that same instant it all became clear in my tortured mind, the rules of this game.

Mentiras, Senor, lies. Of course, there would be no rescue. The moment was colored with treachery, simple yet cunning. They would not allow for this game of hunter and hunted to end quickly or simply. The devious design of it all caused me a bone-deep shudder, like a ship just before it slips beneath the iron-grey waves in a storm.

The *pistola?* It was not loaded, *mi amigo*. It was merely a prop to provide me hope that could be snatched at the right moment in this fetid drama. Hope that could be shattered and the game renewed. Capture and escape. Capture and escape. I would remain forever the pursued, don't you see the grotesque beauty of it all. *Bastardos, todos*.

Bastards, all of them. Oy. *Perdoname, por favor.* And they, it, *la muerte*, death would continue to pursue.

And that, my friend, was the play unfolding. One in which we are all part of. The drama that we, *si, tambien tu*, enact day after day, year after year, until finality. *Y por que?*

Que paso? Well, then all four gathered about me and taunted and provoked me with insults and threatening gestures. Yet, and I don't know why, I felt no reason to respond as they wished and expected I would.

I would run no more. No, friend. *Por que?* To be chased again?

"*Matame!*" I spoke to the one I knew to be the leader. "Kill me here and now and let the game be over." And I spoke clearly with no uncertainty beneath my words, and in the stillness that followed, my entire life compressed itself into a single breath as I knew I stood but a breath apart from mortality. *Sin vida.* And *si*, I did prefer death to this horrific farce.

He in charge nodded to the underlings. They raised their rifles. I closed my eyes and drew my final breath. But relief did not come in the expected torrent of pain and screeching metal. Instead, I heard their armaments clatter to the hard ground, heard scuffling, then yelps and whimpering. And that, senor, summoned up a greater foreboding in my heart than all that had transpired up to this point. *Por dios*, I crossed myself and on opening my eyes *encontre el Maestro de la noche*, the dark master, and even more terrifying his *companeros* transformed into Doberman dogs. Hounds of hell they were, *senor*, and they strained the chains that bound them in their blood lust, for my blood. He, their tender, I could not see as the light had left the sky and all I could make out was a dark robed figure. On both his shoulders, fattened ravens sat and would dart their bloodied beaks into the darkened hooded head, feeding on his maleficent thoughts.

The hounds slathered, bared broken and ragged fangs, and their eyes burned orange in the cold dusk of day. A stench of rotted flesh choked the breath from me, and I made to vomit but could not as I stood paralyzed in dread at the sight of these ungodly brutes. And even now the smell of carrion lingers about me. Do you not smell it, friend?

I strained my vision to catch a glimpse of a face, anything human inside the hooded cassock, but could not. Only smoke emanated from the darkness there and then he, it, spoke in a voice, guttural, bloody, drawn from rack-tortured souls, from the doomed, the oppressed. Your soul is mine, the voice said, and he leveled a bony, yellowed finger my way, and I shall bide my time. And again, that dreadful, dreadful laugh, so sinister and so hollow I shrank away, my courage quickly waning.

And yet I stood my tenuous ground and even though my voice wavered I commanded, "Leave me now dark spirit, *dejame*, the game has ended, for I and I alone will determine my demise. I will summon you at the hour of my choosing and will lie down. And so shall it be done. So leave me now. I will no longer be the sport of your hunt. I will be the pursuer." And I crossed myself again and prayed the prayers of my father. *Si, de mi padre.*

" Fool! You think you have won, taken the pleasure of the hunt from me. I will be back."

I do not know, *mi amigo*, if it was the prayers or my boldness that extricated me from the clutches of that dark messenger, but he turned with a mournful wail that filled the night and transformed my skin to goose flesh, yanked those dreaded hounds about and drifted into the gloom of night until finally only the smell and his fading laugh lingered. What little light remained paled about me, the forest shrank from view, and I found myself once again in total darkness. Where? I do not know.

Ah. But now, *mi amigo*, I am once again in the light of hope. My path is illuminated, and you, *si, tu*, in listening to my story have lit the torch. *Gracias, muchos, mi amigo?* Why do you laugh? Oh. *Dios mio.* That laugh, that horrid, horrid laugh, and that smell. *Por Dios*, no, no, not again.

Chapter 18

Time and Space

Within the collective unconscious of Shamans worldwide, there is the belief that everything consists of vibrational energy and is interconnected, therefore any action can affect the whole or its parts. There is also the understanding of alternate realities and how to access these, and how to navigate space and time. That in healing the past, they heal the present and the future.

Shamans across the millennium have employed sound and vibration, as well as psychogenic plants, to alter consciousness to engage time and space. Thus giving them a broader view of reality. It is through these Shamans that the study of reality, time, and space will be advanced because they have the necessary tools and experience.

Our twenty-first century has advanced rapidly in relationship to technology and all its connections. The amount of knowledge available is so vast; storing it all is a technical challenge. Practically anyone and almost anything can be found by people around the world who know how to access this knowledge. We are unable to keep up with the changes brought about by this development. There are watchdogs, visionaries, scientists, and others studying and working with these vibrational patterns. Shamans fit in with these visionaries. That also means the concerted effort or energy of many can affect the whole in a

Orbiting Earth is a junkyard of debris. The importance of space-based technology cannot be overstated. Disruption and destruction of these systems is sure to follow, and the fallout of those actions will be felt by all. There are 2,000 tracked pieces of debris and a million small pieces in low earth orbit. It is highly possible for collisions to occur causing further collisions and a domino effect to take place rendering most or all space-based technology useless.

The point here is that a Twenty-First Century Shaman's roles and responsibilities have expanded with the demands of this century. One of those roles is the education of the public at large to dispel the television version of the Shaman as a wild rattle-shaking savage, and to share what knowledge they have acquired along the way. We are at the most critical time in our history. It demands an extreme critical response, if we are to reverse this apocalyptic course we are treading upon.

Chapter 19

2016

When I peer into the future with my crow eye, it is a far different world than we now trundle around in, wearing our designer sunglasses and driving one person per military-style vehicle. Based on one known fact, predictions can be made, and inferences assured. That fact is that the world population will soon double. And this doubling time cycle shrinks with each cycle. This one known fact should shake the house of false security like a rolling earthquake. Yet people continue to bear ill-equipped children, blind to world conditions and unarmored, who will have to become warriors if they are to survive.

  There are those who will say that the future is bright, and we are assured of an abundant and stable world. Every sign, every indication point to an overpopulated world with dwindling resources and all the inherent problems associated with those conditions. As of this writing, the world population is 7.9 billion. In approximately thirty short years we will be staring dumbfounded through tear-blurred eyes at approximately sixteen billion mouths to feed. Some of you will still be alive. This is not a doomsday message; it is an eyes wide open to the world condition. Wars, famine, climate changes aside, look closer to the hearth, at the homeless, the hungry struggling to survive all around us. If we cannot provide a solution for a presently manageable number, then the situation can only become a tattered vestment worn by most. I say most because there will always be those who gather the best of the harvest for themselves, and it is a trend seen even now.

What does this information have to do with Shamanism? Everything! Let us return to the concept of everything consisting of vibrations, or Spider's web, or the butterfly phenomena. Shamans dwell in the past, the present, and the future. Twenty-First Century Shaman's roles and responsibilities have expanded in time and space. Farseers are not prophets but are prophetic.

Ignorance is bliss. I do not want to know these conditions, but I do. The web is vibrating at a high and dangerous frequency, and it's difficult to ignore.

Palm oil is a world commodity, a World Wide Web occurrence, a vibration that exists in time and space. I'm using the term "time" as our potential future. This story does not start at the place where the commercial value was realized. Indigenous people had known and used it for generations, primarily in Africa. Palm oil is now the most popular vegetable oil in the world. Palm oil touches the lives of everyone reading these words. It can be found in so many products it would take pages to list its uses. To name a few: a huge number of food products, biodiesel fuel, bread, lipstick, soap, lotions, and dynamite. And yes, the filling in your Oreo cookie. It is listed by various names. It is an incredibly versatile product, which is a good thing, so good that the global consumption is approximately seventy-five million tons. It is produced mainly in Indonesia and Malaysia. Nine hundred thousand acres of deforestation occurs each year due to production of palm oil. Ironically, it is being reintroduced back to Africa where the rain forests there are being decimated to produce palm oil.

Trees do not a rainforest make. Deforestation, cattle ranching, and hunting has resulted in the loss of habitat and the extinction of hundreds of species of animals and plants. Chemical pollution, fossil fuel emissions, CO_2, loss of bees, soil erosion, plastic pollution, polluted oceans are but a few of the many issues demanding our attention. Do I need to go on to stress the urgent need for web shakers? Extrapolate from any one of the earth wounds, and you become a Farseer. The issues are there in blatant view.

Fur Man: From the Cave Gallery sculpture collection.
He evokes strong emotion in viewers.

David Attenborough, a celebrated nature documentarian, narrated *Our Planet*, a filmography that documents the dangers of climate change and loss of biodiversity. With decades of experience and study of our changing planet, he now says, "The question is, are we going to be on time, and are we going to do enough? I don't see the kind of effort needed to affect positive change. We won't be able to do enough to mend everything, but anything that can be done is better than nothing at all." Attenborough does feel there is still time and solutions to the disaster we face. I pray he is right.

A large part of the solution is awareness, an expansion of consciousness. Become a Farseer. Gather a tribe of Farseers, a club, a den, a pack, a murder. Watch *Our Planet*. And when we have gathered enough web shakers, the vibration generated will rumble like thunder across a prairie. Every single person matters when it comes to promoting change because this crisis affects everyone and the immediate future of humanity. Also, we all contribute to the problems. Do not label me as an activist, a prophet, or any such ilk. As a Twenty-First Century Shaman these issues are my concern. My responsibility is to not only bring attention to the overall crisis, but to also encourage the involvement of the village in the solution. The issues and problems of today have complex dynamics, and we don't know the full scope of any one issue. We have virtually exhausted the grains in our hourglass. Your voice matters. Speak up, speak out, and become informed. If only 9 percent of donated plastic is recycled, why recycle? What happens to the other 91 percent? In recycling we contribute 91 percent of the plastic being shipped around the world, and it is either dumped into the ocean or burned. Producers of manufactured plastics take no responsibility for plastic pollution and mislead consumers into believing they are being conscientious by recycling their plastics. We must demand that producers take responsibility for the problem they have created.

Our cultural landscape should also include social issues that affect our future as an evolved species. The decimation of cultures has resulted in the loss of the diverse visions and knowledge accumulated over centuries by people who have managed to survive and flourish where few present-day societies could manage. These people are being told who they are and who they should be, despite having raised families for generations. They already know who they are, and how they fit into the universal picture.

People have heard of the Ghost Dance religion but know little about it. One man, a Paiute Shaman, and his visions created one of the most epochal religious movements in western history. An Eighteenth-Century Shaman, Wovoka, preached the equivalent of Christianity with Paiute mysticism. The movement was brought on by the despair of the Native peoples due to the invading settlers of their lands and decimation of their cultures and dignity. In a final desperate grasp for dignity and survival, this Shaman brought a message of hope to the people.

He spoke of visions that foretold of the world being renewed and the Native people restored to the life they once knew. There would be buffalo, food, warmth, and comfort in place of poverty, hopelessness, and disgrace.

In his visions he received instructions that if they danced the sacred dance, sang the sacred songs, wore the Ghost Dance shirt, and lived the prescribed life, their world would be restored. In three years, the movement spread across the lands to hundreds of tribes and thousands of natives. This one man, Wovoka, had united the entire native population of America in hope of reclaimed dignity and culture.

The Ghost Dance movement was seen as a threat to the government and settlers, even though the native population had been decimated and relocated to reservations, which is made up of land deemed worthless. Mismanaged by the government, the people were forced to live under their control and to depend on them for survival. All treaties negotiated and signed by the government were never kept. The Battle of Bull Run, where General Custer and his company had been defeated by Sitting Bull and a multitude of other plains Indians and chiefs, remained fresh in the minds of the government and settlers. Onlookers had packed picnic baskets to watch that military encounter.

The Dance was banned and participants persecuted, culminating in the massacre at Wounded Knee. This was the death blow to the movement and to the tenuous dignity of an entire population of Natives. It is no accident that Shaman Wovoka is not known to the general public. He and the Ghost Dance religion is relegated to the dark unknown shadow of our history. It remains a bloodstain covered over by the living room carpet. The point here is that one man, this Paiute Shaman, brought the entire native nations together in an epochal movement to save the world as they knew it.

This bit of history is but one example of the shadow, a collective shadow of the only known sentient life in this star-strewn infinity. This is not to imply that the shadow is always malevolent. It is the suppression of anything the human mind does not want to bring into the light for others to examine. It lurks in the basement in the darkest corners shrouded in the webs of denial. The loss of century's worth of knowledge, wisdom, and understanding of who and what we are and our place in the universe is lost as culture after culture is absorbed by modernity.

If it appears I have taken you down a twisted path, going who knows where, that may be, or it may not be. As we stumble into the twenty-first century there will be times of utter horror, spectacular beauty and dignity, and technical and scientific discovery. There are wondrous things we don't know and wondrous things to be discovered. On our walk, you and I have traversed the personal and on through the world village into the past, the present, and the future.

During a shamanic path one of the more relevant processes is that of expanding consciousness. And what that means is going beyond ourselves, beyond our family, friends, nations, the earth, perceived reality. Germs were not a reality not too long ago, and the sun circled the earth. Multiverses are a popular topic of discussion these days. Carlos Castaneda, Shaman and anthropologist, wrote of an alternate reality. Shamans have been studying and working with consciousness and reality for a very long time, and they know of this phenomenon of alternate realities, of spirit worlds where gods and demons and dragons and magicians' dwell. Once these worlds are accessed and experienced, one cannot deny their reality. The following is the continuation of the earlier material related to *Prima Materia* and *Solutio*. In the alchemical process, to proceed further, material must first be reduced to its Prima Materia. Earlier a young man had been put into the black liquid and absorbed. Here is the second part of that earlier dream:

Author's Dream of 1996

I am still in the institution for men. I am standing on a landing of some stairs with a large group of inmates. I am now one of them, dressed in prison clothes and talking to a chunky built inmate. I move to lean against the wall and brush against another prisoner. He becomes angry and reaches into his jacket and pulls out a homemade weapon. It looks like brass knuckles with sharp claws protruding and he attacks me. Others grab him before he can do me harm. I feel anxious and afraid.

The stocky man and I leave the building and are walking in a park-like grounds area and are talking. We leave the prison grounds and are now wearing regular street clothes.

The stocky man walks into a stand of evergreen trees and there transforms into a large muscular, brown, and white bull. I experience extreme fear. The bull begins to attack, and I am at first confused because earlier he had befriended me. I begin to dodge and sidestep his attacks and believe that if I can wrestle it down to the ground, I will be able to contain it. I do manage to throw the bull with extreme effort, but it keeps getting up and attacking. I am exhausted.

Three more bulls, brown and white, appear and charge me. I manage to dodge them or wrestle them down, but it continues, and I realize I can't win by fighting them. I know I cannot withstand another attack.

A voice tells me, "Use your magic!" I understand I must use the power of my mind. Struggling to contain my fear, I call on my discipline and focus my mind on shrinking them. Initially nothing happens, but little by little they begin to shrink then finally disappear. I feel relief.

The voice tells me, "Very good, but let's see what you can do against Stephen King's Monkey Dogs."

A street scene appears, and I am now in a city. It is dusk with some orange light at the horizon.

The shadows are long and dark. The sky has darkened, and the street is cast in eerie shapes and shadows. Buildings line the street on either side.

Against the fading light, I can see Monkey Dogs dashing across the street, howling and screeching as they disappear into the shadows.

I begin to walk up the street feeling no fear. Monkey Dogs leap out of the dark at me, their eyes red and with bone-white fangs. I put my hand out in front of me and said, "Poof!" The Monkey Dogs fall at my feet, turn to fine gray dust, and blow away. I wonder why I am being tested.

Initially I am imprisoned and require others to intervene on my behalf with the attacking man. I gain increased freedom and engage in physical struggle to fend off the attacks by the bulls until I realize this approach is not working. The underlying phenomenon represented by the bulls and my physical struggle with them symbolizes my relationship with my fear, an aspect of my shadow. I overcome the bulls, thus my fear, without any help.

I am then given a final test via Stephen King's Monkey Dogs, who are a further extension of my fear. By extinguishing them using only my powers, I manage to handle my fear and reaffirm my confidence. Finally released from the prison confines, and confident in my powers, I am free.

Chapter 20

Lions, Tigers, and Bears

The question of where we are as a species is pertinent to the Twenty-First Century Shaman because of the implications it has for our future. And once again I speak of the immediate future. As the large land animals become extinct are we humans slated for the same destiny?

    A quick review of some unpleasant facts: The South China tiger is now extinct in the wild with the surviving members held in captivity. There are approximately five hundred Sumatran tigers known to exist. There are approximately forty Amur leopards left in the wilds. Orangutans, turtles, black rhinos, and Sumatran elephants are in danger of becoming extinct. This is just a few of the animals in danger. The palm oil industry is one of those responsible for this issue due to loss of habitat. The rain forests are being decimated at an alarming rate with devastating effects on our climate and wildlife habitat. The loss of any one species influences the entire food chain and ecosystem. The loss of bees would have a profound effect on every living person on the planet. Yet, the chemical industry supported by our elected government continues to pump untold amounts of pesticides into our environment. And just as alarming is that people are using these chemicals and fertilizers to keep their lawns green with the resulting runoff polluting water tables, streams, rivers, oceans, aquifers, and the very air we breathe. Large box stores stock tons of these chemicals for daily use. Once again, we see how we as individuals are contributors to our environmental crisis. Choices are made. My responsibilities along these lines were revealed in the following dreamtime vision.

Author's Dream of 1996

Helena and I are on a military base. I decide I want to go into a top-secret building. It seems to have something to do with some secret energy. I dress in a Colonel's uniform. Helena is also dressed in a uniform.

I approach the guard post and tell them I am Colonel Morris, and I am there to inspect the facility. The guard is suspicious, but I intimidate him, and he allows us to enter.

Helena goes up some stairs and I enter a room with what appears to be an ordinary swimming pool. I do not get in it because I feel it is not safe and decide to leave. On trying the doors, I find I am locked in and become concerned. One of the doors leads to the outside and has a window in it. I catch the attention of someone passing by who in turn alerts the authorities. A man in civilian clothes escorts me out and is walking with me. As we talk it become clear to me that he is going to kill me.

He produces a slingshot and shoots me with a small radioactive pellet, which penetrates my skin near my left groin, then he leaves. As we were walking and talking, he told me he had to kill me because I was entering places I shouldn't enter.

Then I am talking to a group of military and civilian people telling them about something that was concerning them. They seemed to not be part of the established order. I don't know what happened to Helena.

I understood that the man could have killed me immediately instead of at a later time. This delay allowed me time to relate what I knew to others. That the military, the government, or others were the keepers or protectors of the secrets inside or that housed the information or knowledge. Since all I saw was the pool, the pool must be the reservoir of certain knowledge and information.

I understood that it contained knowledge of the downfall of mankind as well as the knowledge of redemption, and that it was my responsibility to bring what information I have to others. There was also a knowing that there are those that would prefer that "things" should not be tampered with that would change the social order.

My visions have guided and steered me in these many directions and have proven to be of profound importance to me and the community at large. It is with that in mind that I venture into what at first may seem to be a tangent, but my role as a Shaman in these times dictates that I venture far and wide in search of truth at the expense of comforting bliss.

The recent scandal regarding wealthy and prominent

people bribing prestigious universities to admit their children brought to mind the following vision I had in dreamtime.

Author's Dream of 1995

There are three well-dressed men and I present. One of these men had cut his finger, a papercut. One of the others produced a styptic pencil and used it on the cut and it did not have time to bleed.

I am using a knife to cut something and cut my finger, a small wound. The man who had first cut his finger saw this and told me, "Quick, use my cut doctor." The "cut doctor" applied the pencil to my finger, and it stopped bleeding.

The third man was working on a computer. He showed me a timeline that could be edited like a film editing program I had used. There was a thin break in the timeline, and he closed it. He explained that we have this timeline where everything is recorded by "tags" in our body. This line is important because it is used in every transaction that we make. It contains our complete health or physical record as well as our behavior. It is accessed when we apply for credit, insurance, purchase a home, etc., and determines the price and eligibility of these transactions.

The computer man explained that insignificant events like the cut finger can be removed from the timeline if done immediately. The desired goal was to have the best timeline possible. And the whole setup was designed so that wealthy people were able to have specialty experts construct a better timeline than those without the experts.

Well into the twenty-first century, we have witnessed extraordinary advancements in every aspect of our lives. Technology today is staggering in its complexity and application. The ability to alter our very DNA and to clone and create designer babies is now a reality, and there are institutions engaged in that very procedure. Despite restrictions and regulations, the work goes on in government and privately supported laboratories around the world.

What are the implications for a not-too-distant future with limited resources for a majority of the world population with average or lower income? It is evolution at an accelerated rate of development controlled by the wealthy and cannot be curbed.

In the early nineties, a coalition of various disciplines gathered at my home at intervals to discuss issues of interest or importance to the members. One of these issues was evolution as it was understood at that time. The outcome of this topic was that we as a species were hardly evolved as seen by the events in our social, political, economic, and related systems.

The discussion of conscious evolution was presented as a necessity to our short- and long-term survival. This discussion applied not only to the human species but also the planetary ecosystem in its entirety. The term Homo Noetikos was the name chosen for the next species in evolution that would represent a shift toward conscious evolution of the human species. I presented the term and the concept at an international conference hosted by the University of Denver for academics, practitioners, and students to collaborate for change. The conference was titled Dialogue, Culture, and Conflict. I was invited to open and close the conference and to speak in my role as Shaman. Since that time, there has been considerable discussion regarding conscious evolution as a solution to our current global and personal problems. We have reached the critical threshold in so many arenas that we will soon see the effects quite clearly. We are losing a million species every year, including plants, insects, sea life, and land animals. Ecosystems and habitats are greatly endangered, and all this is attributed to man's activities and population growth.

Expanded consciousness is one of the goals and results of shamanic practices, but it is a two-sided coin. Ignorance is bliss, but at what price? The price is our future, the future of children being born now into a future that holds no hope of peace, security, happiness, and many of the freedoms we take for granted.

The adage "change is the only constant" is true in relation to people and civilizations. What is different is the rate of change and that we now find ourselves in the midst of exponential change never before experienced. Long ago, I had felt that the scenario in one of my dreams addressed the issue of change and had been compelled to record it with sketches.

Author's Dream of 1994

Driving in a car with Helena, and we come upon a police car with its doors open, parked on a side street. I walk over to the car and find two police officers sprawled in the front seat. They have been shot and are dead.

Nearby on a vacant lot, a building begins to self-form, brick by brick into a two-story building. I stand and watch it until it has completed itself. I do find it both odd and fascinating. Equally as interesting to me is that people show no interest in that event.

We drive away to look for a phone to report what we had witnessed. We encounter an unmarked police car and a plainclothes detective or what I perceive as an authority figure. I flag him down and begin to tell him what was happening. He stated that he already knew what was happening as he had received several calls about it. Yet he appeared unconcerned. We drive away.

Then I am on the roof of a building looking out over the city. In the distance another building begins to self-form. It is also of brick and roughly oval at its base. The bricks are spiraling, piling layer on layer until a certain height is reached. Poles or pillars shoot up from one end of the oval and another section begins forming on top of the pole. As it grows in height with more poles and more oval sections, people become frightened.

The shapes that form at the top of each pole vary. I realize that it should topple due to its seemingly unbalanced structure. It grows continually until it disappears into the clouds instead. I can see it begin to lean.

Then the buildings between that structure and the one I am on begin to crumble and collapse into dust in a widening circle away from the new structure. There are people on some of these roofs, and they go with the collapsing buildings.

Someone yells for everyone to get out of the building we are on. The wave of collapsing buildings approaches in a rolling gray cloud of dust. Everyone is scrambling to get off the roof.

Someone says the event is caused by a child. I understand that an extraordinary child has been born and is indeed creating these buildings and is causing the collapse of the others.

I ask, "Am I being given another story to write?"

I am told, "No! The story of the child did not begin here or now."

THE WAY OF THE CROW

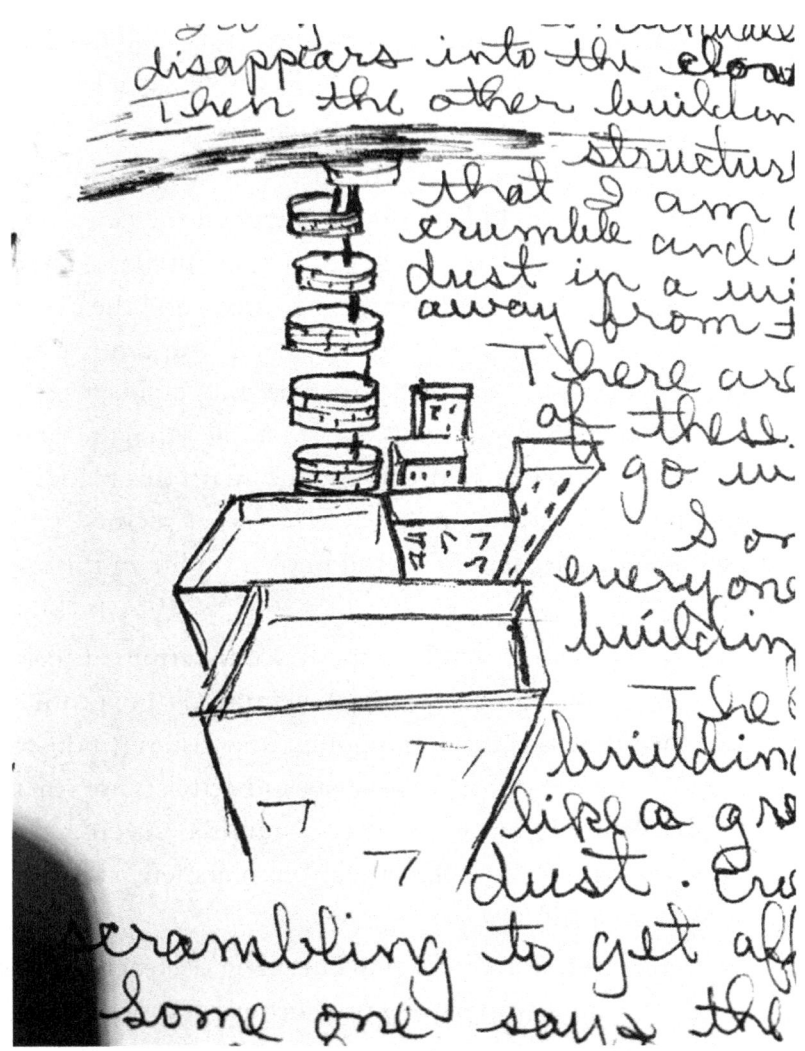

Sketch from 1994 observing rapid changes in social structures.
The child represents the era of breakdown.

Upon analyzing the dream, I have concluded the following. The police who were shot are an indication of the breakdown in order, which many people are aware of but are unconcerned by.

The social structure, the first self-forming building, begins to manifest but is still somewhat conventional. Still, people are not taking notice. Then the process of change hastens and is quite evident and of consequence. The child is a new era and has its roots in the past. The child being born is indeed the cause of the new social structures and the collapse of the buildings, the old order. If we peer with eyes wide open, the chinks and the decay of our lives lived in denial will flare like a supernova. And unfortunately, many lives will be lost as the child reaps the whirlwind of change that is upon us. Most people can name at least one disastrous condition that affects the future on this planet. But if they understand it is just one piece of a larger picture, people will gain a greater awareness of its full impact on life in this room we call earth.

As a result, people will become more determined to right the unguided actions of global financial institutions, governments, education, agribusiness, farming, logging, and fishing industries. Threats against environmental journalists and activists are real and deadly. Global Witness reports that two hundred seven activists were killed in 2017 due to their involvement in global investigations of harmful practices.

Awareness is a primary step in curtailing destruction of the planet. As the awareness expands, pressure can be put on those entities responsible for detrimental practices. We become the web shakers, the Farseer, the activists, a formidable force to be reckoned with in the face of opposition. The danger to activists is real and at times subtle. It is imperative that one enter this engagement with this firmly understood.

I have taken you on an ever-expanding circle of information related to the Twenty-First Century Shaman's worldview in hopes of dispelling misconceptions and offering enlightenment, not only about the practitioner, but also about certain issues vital to our very existence.

Chapter 21

Spirituality vs Religion

I will define religion as a cultural organization centered on a prescribed system of shared beliefs and practices, comprised of adherents to those shared views. Whereas spirituality is an individual experience of beliefs and practices. If asked, "What is your religion?" One could respond with some denomination. One can experience spirituality within the context of the prescribed belief system and be both religious and spiritual.

The image that lingers with me is of a lone elderly woman dressed in black, her bowed head covered in a scarf, kneeling in a church, the silence heavy about her, the only sounds the rattling of her rosary beads passing through arthritic fingers. One can sense she is in a spiritual endeavor. Spirituality involves the experiences that promote transcendence, a view of the wonder and awe of not only who we are but of the whole of existence without explanation. Creation exists independent of man's thoughts about it. Man did not create the existence of the universe. Man is a creation of the existence of the universe.

The desert is a cathedral. When one can view the expanse of night sky from horizon to horizon and peer into infinity, one cannot help but feel awe. It is the realization of the immensity of creation and the minuteness of the I. This is the presence of God. It is infinite, without beginning and without end. It has always been and always will be. One realizes the insignificance of who and what we are as we stand before our creator. It causes me to fall to my knees and weep.

Chapter 22

The Gaia Hypothesis

What I'd Rather Not Know

One of the most influential scientists of our time, James Lovelock, developed the Gaia Hypotheses many decades past. It states that the earth is a massive, self-regulating organism. Many believe this, and we see some important evidence of that observation. It bears repeating that I am neither an activist nor an alarmist. My position is one of an intermediary. It is imperative in this emerging Novacene era that expanded consciousness accompanies the superintelligence of our planet. One without the other is a two-legged stool.

The import of this information is that it affects everyone, some sooner than others. With grim satisfaction, I know I will be deceased as we stumble blindly into an apocalyptic future. Knowledge and information are power, and information is now the most valuable commodity in the world economy. The amount of information being bought and sold, and the money involved is staggering. There are some five thousand to ten thousand data points in cyberspace for every living individual. This information is used to influence, to guide, and to manipulate the unwary.

Population explosion continues unabated. Children born during this time are facing an unimaginable scenario of haves and have nots as scant resources of all types come under the control of the privileged few. If people knew and believed this, would they continue to bear children? How can these children cope with this world? Can or will parents prepare their children for this world? I share these insights in hopes that people will not only make informed choices but also in hopes of a mass movement to give the children a future.

The Fellowship Foundation, also known as The Family, is an organization of the elite and powerful world leaders who operate under the guise of the teachings of Jesus. They operated under the doctrine of secrecy for many years, with the belief that their work could best be served covertly. An overriding principle of that group is that these world leaders have been chosen by God and will be guided by God. Trump had proclaimed he was The Chosen One. This is not a conspiracy theory. This information is now readily available to anyone wishing to pursue the truth. And what is the plight of those who are not among the chosen? Their objective is a new world order overseen by the "Chosen!"

The Amazonian rain forest is being decimated by deforestation, logging, or burning for the use of agriculture and cattle. The rapid rate of this process is visible via satellite imagery. Yet, it continues despite its known detriment to the planet, and its ineffective use of nonexpendable resources. Not only does it degrade the carbon cycle, but the fires also add to the CO_2 pollution. Most days the air quality is reported as poor in my area. Rainforests have a delicate ecosystem of plants and animals. The plants have adapted to the fragile soil conditions of the rainforest, which is not conducive to agriculture. That soil is quickly depleted, and further deforestation is inevitable.

Rainforest animals do not adapt to destruction of their habitat. The encroachment from all around them greatly reduces the amount of territory available to sustain their viability. The loss of the rainforests far outweighs the benefits. Cattle ranching requires a huge expenditure of resources better directed to a growing need to feed impoverished and desperate multitudes.

Twenty-five percent of the planet's countries are suffering severe water shortages. Presently, fresh water is a growing concern for all. The aquifers are drying up and are being polluted. The oceans are polluted with toxic waste and plastic. The microplastics have found their way into the food chain. Seventy-three percent of fish in the Northwestern Atlantic have plastic in their digestive systems. More than half the Great Barrier Reef off Australia is blanched and dead, the other half is in danger. Other reefs are facing the same demise and with their destruction there goes an important element of the ocean's ecosystem.

As unsettling as all this is to me, it is my responsibility to inform those who will spread the information and will become part of the solution. In other words, those who will bring about change for the survival of all the planets inhabitants. It saddens me to peer into the future, and the course we are on terrifies me. It is the burden of the Twenty-First Century Shaman to face reality with eyes wide open. We are engaged in a time of trial and tribulation of biblical proportions.

What can be done? The power of the masses is a formidable influence. Become informed, expand consciousness, become a Farseer, recruit other Farseers, vote intelligently with an eye on the future because the future is now everywhere present. To become a Farseer all one must do is take on any one ongoing crisis and examine the implications to their fullest. I repeat this because of its importance to all. The world population doubles approximately every thirty years. We are coming up on eight billion presently. Do the math. I recall with clarity in 1960 when that number was three billion.

If I am soon to be deceased, why should I burden myself? I have children, who have children is the reason, and that is why everyone should take notice. We owe it to them. What I hear from certain sectors is that things will turn around, we need to have faith, have positive thoughts, don't dwell on the world crises. If there is one thought I would want the reader to take away from this, it is this, and I repeat:

> As long as there is hope,
> there is no hope.
> When there is no hope,
> then there is hope.
> Hope is the great deceiver.

The point being that when the illusion of hope is obvious then action will be taken. Take this message and repeat it often and to as many people as possible. I wish for it to spread around the world. The message came to me during a meditation session, and I understood the truth of it. And I do understand the reluctance of people to believe what I have been saying, because as I look out my window, I see a peaceful world of trees and a flower dappled yard, birds, rabbits, and a quiet neighborhood. But if I really look, I can also see the war-torn countries, the displaced refugees, the hungry, and all the underlying bits and pieces of a deteriorating world beyond my neighborhood.

Keep in mind that we live in a one room house, and it is getting smaller daily. I cringe as I write and read these words wanting instead to entertain, to encourage hopefulness, to provide sustenance to a hungry mind. Instead, mine is to armor you for the upcoming time of darkness descending upon us. It matters not whether you believe it. Unless you are part of the chosen one percent, we will all be storming the same gates.

I have taken you on a journey from the microcosm to the macrocosm in hopes of activating that spark of interest or defiance, to convince you to act in whatever way you can to nudge the future in a direction that is conducive to harmony and prosperity. I for one do not want to wait until there is no hope. There are more questions inferred here than answers, so if anyone has answers please share them. Our future depends on you.

Chapter 23

Call Me Kikta

Joseph High Eagle, a Lakota Medicine man, gave me my spirit name, *Kita Ota Wanaji*, which means Awakens Many Spirits, on my fiftieth birthday. It is the most meaningful gift I have ever received. A remarkable man, he walked in two worlds, both the spiritual and the profane with equal ease. A white boy taken in and raised to adolescence on a reservation by the Black Elk clan, he incorporated the culture and the sacred underpinnings of his spiritually rich exposure. Removed from the only family he knew at an early age, he found himself relocated to the East with a white family who raised him in a caring and positive environment. After many years he had adapted to a white man's world and culture.

Intelligent and resourceful, he had acquired an education and had spent his adult life in academia. On retirement he had migrated to the Four Corners area of Mancos, Colorado, and had integrated with ease into the spiritual community, becoming a respected spiritual elder. There came a time when word was received from the Western slope that Joseph was ill, stricken with cancer. Divided by the Rocky Mountains, the Eastern slope and the Western slope communities were in communication and were well known to each other. They often worked in cooperation.

With the ill-fated news regarding Joseph and keeping in mind my spirit naming gift, I decided it would be appropriate and meaningful to perform an honoring ceremony to thank him for his many services to the community. I called Joseph's wife to inform her of my intentions and asked her to inform the community. In response, many Shamans and other practitioners then gathered there from various locales to pay respects to this man. I traveled there with my wife to shepherd this event, not anticipating the obstacles I would encounter in this seemingly honorable gesture. When I arrived at Mancos, I discovered discord within the community and animosity directed toward me by the resident Shaman, a powerful woman practitioner. A power struggle broke out between us.

On the day prior to arriving at Mancos, I had conducted a ceremony in Trinidad, Colorado, and then proceeded to the Four Corners that evening. Arrangements had been made for me and my wife to meet community members at the resident Shaman's home for a gathering and planning session. On arrival, the community greeted us warmly. They expressed interest and were supportive of my earlier day's activities. Meanwhile, the resident Shaman had not acknowledged me and sat off to one side knitting. As I began to approach her, after greeting the other guests, she said, "Humm, it sounds like a Salvation Army show to me," and kept on knitting. The other guests were stunned into silence. Helena quickly came to my rescue as did others.

After some tense interactions with her in which she continued to discount me, the offending issue came out. I had transgressed a territorial protocol by not informing her and planning the ceremony with her prior to my arrival. My plan had been to do this when I met with her at her home. Once she understood and accepted what I explained to her, we were able to set a breakfast meeting for the following morning to work out the details of the ceremony and further clear the air.

The next day at breakfast concessions had to be discussed and agreed upon. The Shaman put forth that I would agree to do an honoring ceremony for her in the fall. She understood that I was in good standing with the community and the ceremony in her name would bolster her faltering position. There were rumors that she had been misusing her authority to take advantage of others' energy and time.

With plans put forth and agreements understood, all arrangements fell into place. I agreed she would play a central role in the ceremony for Joseph the following day. We also agreed the Rocky Mountains would be the dividing line demarcating our respective territories. I was designated the Eastern slope, and she the Western slope. We were to confine our practice to those territories unless otherwise agreed upon by mutual consent.

The following day broke generously pleasant, the late spring weather warm and sunny. The community responded with enthusiasm in support of the occasion with food and musicians, and all seemed to be going well, grudges and resentments put aside. The resident Shaman played host and was in her element directing activities through the course of the event. During a circle dance, Joseph got up and joined the participants. He began the shuffling circling movement, and then began a warrior's dance to the amazement of the gathering. The resident Shaman became concerned due to Joseph's age and medical condition and rushed over to him to support and manage his enthusiasm. On returning to his seat, he radiated energy and keenness, and appeared transformed in a positive form.

The event was well received, and there were many comments regarding how the community had needed this event to bring the community together again. The guests retired as the sun set in glorious color to the west. Joseph's wife motioned me over. In a whispered voice she told me the cancerous lesion Joseph had on his chest had fallen off. I later learned that he felt he had reverted to his true self, the Lakota self of his youth.

The following day he appeared energetic and enthusiastic about a wedding he was to officiate that day. The wedding took place in a large kiva known only to the local residents. Joseph appeared in full ceremonial dress, and it was evident that he stood in his power and grace. Joseph had returned home.

The wedding ceremony officiated by Joseph High Eagle. Accompanied by Helena on flute and Antonio on drums.

That fall, as agreed upon, the honoring ceremony for the Western slope Shaman was organized, and the community gathered for the event. Generous speeches were made and copious amounts of food consumed. Amends made and grievances forgiven, the gathering proceeded in a festive mood.

During this ceremony, the Shaman announced she would be retiring to pursue other interests and would be relinquishing her position in the community. To my surprise, she presented me with her talisman, her symbol of authority. The season passed, and the following year I received notice that Joseph had passed on. It was a major loss to that community and to me in particular.

Chapter 24

The Return of Merlin

The Wizard of Kansas had provided me critical information regarding care of the sword he had bestowed on me. I did not heed his words, and they returned to haunt me with disastrous consequences.

During the ceremony for Joseph, I had used the sword and noticed something unsettling about it. Blood-colored streaks ran down both sides of the blade. Rust was eating away at it. I had failed to care for it properly. The Wizard's words and instructions for its care echoed forth to haunt me.

On returning home I searched for and found a knifemaker. I inquired if he could restore the blade. He informed me he could "glass bead it" and that would take care of the problem. I left it in his care and returned home to consider my folly. I had not regarded it as a sacred piece and had not cared for it as such, so I felt not worthy of wielding it. Further events reinforced that insight.

A week later I retrieved the sword from the knifemaker, experiencing relief in anticipation of the sword being restored and vowed to care for it as instructed by the Wizard from Kansas. The knifemaker handed me a paper-wrapped package. I tore at the wrappings and the gleaming gold handle with glistening black rainbow obsidian inlay revealed itself. I slid the paper wrapping from the blade. When I saw the blade, I became dumbstruck. The blade had been transformed into a gray matte surface the color of ash that resembled a plastic toy. Speechless, I left the shop bearing the paper-wrapped sword. For years it then lay hidden away on a shelf, where I had placed it, unable or unwilling to face the result of my carelessness.

Years later, while sitting in a coffeeshop reading Deepak Chopra's *The Return of Merlin*, I came upon a passage where the woman in a green felt hat tells Arthur to "look carefully through the ashes." A house had burned to the ground. Arthur does not know what he is looking for, but as he sweeps his hands through the ashes, they bite upon an object which he pulls from the rubble. He recognizes it as a scabbard and instantly knows that what he is seeking is Merlin's sword. The significance of the ashes and the ash-colored blade struck me as an directive. I was to recover it from its ashen state.

At that instant I was struck by the realization that what I had was indeed a mythical Merlin's sword. My first response was, "Oh Lord, why me?" The true meaning of the initial vision of the sword became clear. I then understood that my sword had indeed been pulled from a stone, an AV (altered vibration) stone tool fashioned by the sculptor and Shaman, Hank Smith. The golden handle inlaid with lapis lazuli and the dark rainbow obsidian stone, and the reason it was to be forged by the hand of a man with a pure heart became clear. Its true meaning is the magic contained in it. In a later meditation, I asked, "What do I do with it?" The answer was, "Wield it. It is a symbol of power and authority."

I dug out the ashen-colored sword determined to right my wrong and researched how to restore it. The information proved helpful and with patience and much polishing the first glimmer of hope shown through. Each day's work brought renewed vision as the blade began to come alive. Finally, the sword emerged resurrected with renewed energy and with a fuller appreciation of what I had renewed as well.

The sword became an integral instrument in my pantheon of sacred objects used during various rituals and ceremonies. Participants understood and accepted the energy of this piece. It was a concrete manifestation of myth and an actualization of manifestation beyond conceptual rhetoric.

Mythology plays itself out in various ways and is still an active component of our human experience. It reflects our connection to our past and can help us understand ourselves as a unified whole.

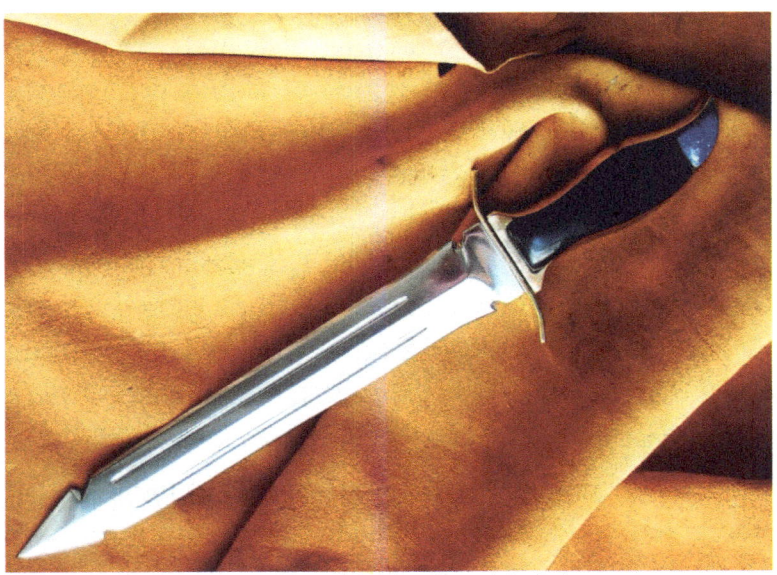

Sword back to its original glory.

Chapter 25

Self-Destruction

Our journey brings us full circle to the issue of climate change and our collective role. The term collective is appropriate in that there is a collective responsibility for our current situation. Among the many factors is capitalism as the source of abundance and the means of our destruction. We have left behind the Anthropocene era and are well entrenched in what is known as the Novacene era. This is the era characterized by extreme knowledge and unfathomable access to information. Yet, we are set on a course of self-destruction from known sources and unwilling to accept that fact. Within ten years, and at the present rate of consumerism, an uncontrollable chain reaction will be set in motion that will have a profoundly devastating effect on the inhabitants of the earth.

The need for raw materials for all aspects of industry that produce the goods and services demanded by our lifestyles have led to deforestation practices that deplete the carbon absorbing rain forests and wildlife habitat of our fellow inhabitants. Mining and agriculture are pouring chemicals and metals into the water systems. Fresh water accounts for only three percent of the world's water. Giant aquifers are drying up. Hydroelectric dams are nonproducing due to inadequate water supplies. Drought and its consequences are a prevalent condition for increasingly vast areas of the world. Water restrictions are in our near future.

Americans use approximately eighty gallons of water per person each day, double the amount used in most other nations. It is important that we become aware of not how much one uses but how much one wastes. If we reduce consumption by ten gallons a day and multiply that by a million people, it will make a significant impact.

CO_2 levels continue to rise despite a call for reduction. What is needed to avert a crisis is zero emissions. Meanwhile, the melting of the Arctic permafrost is releasing huge amounts of trapped CO_2. The melting is a result of climate change.

The most basic needs for survival of the human species are land, air, and water. All these elements are rapidly being degraded to the point of pollution and depletion. The world's oceans are overfished. Plastic pollution has crept into every level of the ocean ecosystem and is passed on to the consumers of ocean products. Microparticles of plastic are now found in our water and in the air we breathe. There is an estimated eight million metric tons of plastic debris that ends up in our oceans. Soon the oceans will, by weight, have more plastic than fish. Plastics eventually break down, releasing chemicals such as bisphenol A, (BPA), that are known to cause health problems for marine life. The food chain leads to humans consuming toxic and carcinogenic pollutants. As I mentioned earlier, approximately only 9 percent of recycled plastic actually gets recycled. Tons of our plastic are shipped around the world on barges looking for countries to accept it. An increasing number of countries are refusing our waste. Much of it is burned, and much of it is dumped into the ocean. That implies that for every ten pieces of our plastic we recycle, one is usable, and nine pieces enter the environment. The producers of plastic have created the myth that to recycle is environmentally responsible while disregarding the reality of what is occurring.

The biosphere is a small room we share with the world. It

extends five miles up and to the depths of the ocean. This is not an infinite space we inhabit. When the forests of Malaysia are burned for palm oil production, we breathe in that pollution. And when we consume all the products that contain palm oil, we are the polluters. As the population explodes, the demand for more palm oil demands more production and more deforestation.

This brings us back to capitalism and our role in that dynamic. As consumers of the products of capitalism we are the engine of the very process that is the instrument of our demise. Human activity has not only altered our lives in negative ways, but it has also altered the climate and the planet on which we depend. Presently, air pollution causes seven million premature deaths at the cost of five billion dollars. This is one of the greatest unseen and unacknowledged health threats we face.

It is a monumental undertaking to affect the worldwide process of weather, yet we have been doing so at a breakneck pace. If this sounds like an alarmist's utterings, know that my voice is but one among many that cry out for our attention and action. If we want to survive as a species, we best respond in earnest.

Chapter 26

COVID-19

The issues of concern are often thought of as individual unconnected problems. When in reality these issues are all interrelated, and each has its own complex set of complications and effects, such as health, social, environmental, economic, political, philosophical, and even religious. They are as a stew in the same cauldron from which we partake of for our sustenance. To only consider the CO_2 problem or the plastic issue, for example, is a limited perspective, one that the French refer to as *esprit de clocher*. This term was derived from medieval times when people did not move from the area where they were born, thus their worldview was only what could be seen from the church steeple. Hence the origin of *esprit de clocher* was used to mean narrowminded. The situation we are facing is much too complex to be resolved with a solution derived from a narrowminded perspective. It is truly a Gordian knot, a complex problem that requires a bold solution.

It is not my intent to terrify or cause panic but to alert a populous used to a way of life that afforded a reasonable view of the future for their children and grandchildren. We now stand at the brink of time when the quicksand beneath the feet of reason is shifting. And it's not as though we have not had notice, predictions, and data that indicated the direction we were heading.

Most of us are sitting in isolation due to the coronavirus. For the first time in U.S. history, every state is under a disaster declaration. The world is facing an uncontrolled pandemic. As of this writing, there have been 261.4 million known cases in the World and 5.2 million known deaths. Doctors and medical staff are understaffed, undersupplied, and are dealing with increased frustration that so many are engaged in self-destructive behaviors despite preventative information and resources. This is another instance of humanity's self-destructive behavior that is difficult to manage or understand.

Here is a piece of fiction written in my journal in 1999, twenty-two years ago, that reflects the present state of affairs in the world today.

"This confirms it, Vaughn, we're in trouble. Big trouble." Martin stared at the monitor displaying the World Biological Research Center's corporate logo, and slowly shook his head.

Vaughn studied his colleague's face. "You don't mean…"

Martin pressed his fingers to his eyes, then nodded.

Vaughn scanned the screen and the glowing dots scattered randomly over a virtual world map. "We've seen this pattern before. It looks like the 2015 scare. It's in the extreme normal range, but we've been here before."

"Yes, yes I know. But there have been significant inroads toward control by then. What's happening in the lab, Vaughn? Any solid leads?"

"No, nothing definite. It has a lot of characteristics of that Asian profile, five years ago, remember?"

"This is different, Vaughn. The dispersal patterns, the growth rate, something. Here, look at this growth rate as compared to our last four most problematic outbreaks, including the Asian thing." He brought up a new screen and watched as the bell curves traced themselves quietly into place. "And that's not all. Look at these." Figures and graphs settled into place.

Vaughn leaned into the monitor, sighed, and shifted the display with two quick keystrokes. He loosened his tie, his brow furled.

"Our European office came up with the same projected infection and mortality figures, Vaughn. We've never had these kinds of figures before." They stood silently staring at the darkened monitor. "Do you pray, Vaughn?"

Rest assured, this is not End Times or Armageddon, although these monikers will surely be added to the "stew" for a more toxic concoction. References will be made to biblical and other quotable sources. The truth is that there is a reality to what is being quoted. The baby has been born and an era of unrest is unfolding. The presently ongoing pandemic is a prelude to the Novacene era into which we are stumbling like an awkward unsuspecting child.

We can expect an outpouring of religious fervor. There will

be proclamations of punishment from God for every conceivable political, social, and personal viewpoint. There will be many who will fall into the clutches of extremists. There is no uncertainty in my mind that we will experience difficult times, but it is a manmade disaster. That said, there can also be manmade solutions. My role is to prepare people and to mobilize resources in preparation for the travails that lie ahead. In that vein I call on practitioners of every occupation to become Shamans and Farseers. The first step is to become aware of where we are in our evolution and then where we are headed. Once we understand that, it will take a concerted effort to manage the crisis and that every bit of energy put into that effort is necessary. Every person alive will be affected, so it's in our mutual interests that every person be involved in seeking and providing solutions at every level possible.

As one wanders through the following scenarios, one can't help but feel the heavy responsibility placed on each of us. The weight is enormous. Keep in mind as these pages unfold with tales of the potential apocalypse that there has been some positive movement by governments and organizations. They are seeking solutions and remedies to all these conditions, recognizing that they and we also hold a responsibility for the causes and the solutions to a developing world crisis that affects all of us equally.

Chapter 27

The Return Home

It is not my intent to examine or explore the Shamans of the world in their various roles in history as this has been done by psychologists, sociologists, ethnologists, philosophers, and the theologians. The vast collection of information is of great value, and the scholarly approach is impeccable. But, in many cases, the studies have been limited to their chosen perspective and to the archaic practices and cultures. I hope to add an updated perspective through my personal experience.

Cultures and societies have undergone dramatic disruptions due to technological and other modern influences. We have witnessed profound advances and global changes that are not necessarily in the best interests of humanity or the planet and its other inhabitants. During the transformation, Shamanism has also had to adapt to the needs of the technological world. The practitioner must incorporate the knowledge of the past and the reality of the present with an eye of the impact on the future. The Twenty-First Century Shaman has an important role to play in the survival of all who inhabit the planet. It is a vastly expanded global role that not every practitioner has taken on, opting instead to practice in the more archaic role. With that in mind, I would like to return to the personal.

C. G. Jung's archetypes can often be observed in the

unconscious realms of the psyche during dreamtime and psychotherapy. The archetypes considered the most prevalent and influential are the Animus, Anima, and the Shadow. These archetypes have deep-rooted origins in the early development of the psyche, particularly ones involving the mother and father. Archetypes are much more complex than I have presented here, and I have endeavored to introduce the most basic nature of these psychic structures. Alchemical processes and alchemy are also presented at a rudimentary level here. There are entire books written regarding these functions as well as the studies of the phenomenon of shamanic practices, so it is not my intent to add to those collections but rather to bring to light the present-day practice and purpose of the Twenty-First Century Shaman. The threads of those historical practitioners are woven inextricably into the cloak with which we now have attired ourselves. One can spend a lifetime in pursuit of an understanding of the arcane practices and the symbolism of these subjects.

When we speak of wholeness, we are referring to all that makes up the human experience. The integration of the facets of one's Self is a lifelong endeavor, consciously or unconsciously. The myths, the archetypes, and dreams are manifestations of the universal quest for enlightenment.

The Quest is for another level of individuation and wholeness in the quester's life. The quester usually is not aware that the events unfolding are, in fact, a myth unfolding. But if one were to examine the events, they would discover the process for what it is, the Hero's Journey.

What precipitated the quest? It was a question. Not just any question, but the right one that set the quest in motion. So, if it was not the right question, the quest would not be set into action. If it is the right question, first there will be the call. The individual is usually called to the Hero's Journey at different stages of their lives, when they are lost and in need of direction, like Dante's hero in the Divine Comedy (Hollander translation), who starts off his journey by saying:

> "Midway in the journey of our life
> I came to myself in a dark wood
> For the straight way was lost."

And so began the call to his long and arduous journey.

The hero can either refuse the call or accept it. If the hero refuses, they will remain stuck in the stage they are at in their life when they received the call. Once the call is accepted, the individual must pass through the gates, which may well entail confronting guardians who are there to test them.

When the individual passes through the gates, they move on to cross the threshold that beckons to them and finally enters the second phase of initiation where they may well meet their mentor, guide, or ally who will provide supernatural aid. In this phase the hero is thrust onto the road of trials and quests where they undertake many ordeals that they encounter along the way.

Events will unfold that will thrust the seeker along a path to an unknown destination. The trials, tribulations, and the responses will dictate the outcome. Along the road of trials, the hero will encounter enemies, allies, and tests. If the hero persists and can survive the ordeals then the reward, the treasure will be secured, but the return of the hero may still require rescue from without. So even in the return there will be obstacles to overcome, ordeals to face. If the Hero returns, they will arrive "home," the place where they belong in this stage of their life. The hero becomes the master of his world and gains freedom to live their life as they choose.

The story of Odysseus demonstrates that journey in a comprehensive unfolding of the bold adventure and has endured the test of time, which speaks to its validity as a shining signpost pointing us in the direction of wholeness. The ancient Sumerian

Myth of Inanna, mentioned earlier, unfolds in a similar fashion as do others which lead one to recognize the enduring power of myth and the archetypes in our lives.

As we traverse the terrain of existence, we encounter other myths and archetypes and utilize them and alchemical processes in our movement toward wholeness. Micro versions of these great dramas are reflected in movies and books, and they mirror the underlying patterns of life. Much of what has been presented here is of an illusionary nature. That is because what we are working with is at a multidimensional level. Shamans have, for centuries, delved into the realms of alternative universes or realities and utilized the energies that sustain them independent of our comprehension and beliefs. The picture is clouded by consciousness, behavior, culture, education, and a host of other influences.

Chapter 28

Burn This One

"*Quemarse lo este pocito*," Lily said to the Tita, an elderly community leader and Shaman who lived high in the Ecuadorian Andes.

I became acquainted with Lily during an exchange program initiated by a professor who opened a church and school for the study and practice of spiritual growth. On her initial visit to the United States, Lily and I exchanged knowledge and the techniques we employed in our respective practices. Lily was an accomplished and well-known Shaman in her community in Ecuador.

During Lily's visit, we established a bond of friendship and acceptance. I had become interested in filmmaking at the time and working with Lily I saw an opportunity to produce some footage of various ceremonies and rituals. On approaching Lily with the idea, she did not feel that it would be appropriate to film these events, nor did anyone else. I was discouraged but determined to find a way to do my filming of these rituals.

The following year she returned, and I again broached the subject with the idea that these practices and cultures are fast disappearing, and it would be a good idea to preserve them. She tentatively agreed with the provision that the prevailing Ecuadorian Shaman performing the ceremony in question would also agree. I later traveled to Ecuador, equipment packed and ready to do my documentary on the Shamans and rituals of

Ecuador.

Ecuadorian Shaman Lily and Antonio performing a shamanic ceremony.

On arrival in Quito, Ecuador, Lily informed me that the Amazon River was still flooded, and we would not be able to travel to visit the Shaman we intended to visit in the jungle there. The Amazon has a major impact on the daily life of the country. As the Amazon floods, it stirs up waste of animals and humans, and diseases. Also, the jungle Shaman had contracted several diseases and had to be airlifted out to a hospital.

We formulated an alternative plan to go up the Andes mountains to see the Tita. He is the spiritual leader of his community and one of the oldest Shamans in that area. But first he had to be contacted via their communications route, which was to contact a friend, who would contact a cousin, and so on, and then wait for the response. Many days later we learned the Tita would see us and would perform a cleansing and purification ceremony with us.

We traveled from Quito to a small town called Otavalo and went to the marketplace there to purchase needed items for the ceremony. We purchased eggs, various alcohols, flowers, several lengths and bundles of greens, candles, cigarettes, and cigars, all to be used in the ceremony. The highways or roads up into the Andes are minimally maintained, and the farther you travel into the mountains the rougher and more treacherous it becomes. We managed to find our way to our destination only to find that the Tita was not there, even though we had been informed he would be there. The eighty-five-year-old Shaman was off tending to livestock. He did arrive later and appeared to be his stated age but displayed vigor and sharpness of mind. We followed him into a large unfinished cement block building, with dirt floors, no lights with rough low wooden seating at the periphery. His grandson, a young man, assisted him in setting up the event and assisted during the nightlong ceremony. Also present were an assistant and several small children. One who was fascinated by my camera equipment sat beneath the tripod watching the events with intense bright eyes. Our party consisted of a dozen participants from around the world who had gathered in Ecuador.

The Tita arranged an altar over a warped piece of weathered plywood using the articles we had brought with us. On completion he had created a beautiful altar with a carpet of greenery and flower petals then placed stones, the eggs, and sprinkled nutmeg on it. Initially, being high in the Andes, the space was chilly, and we kept our jackets on to ward off the brisk night air.

Ecuador has an abundance of hot springs due to the volcanic activity and many of our previous rituals and ceremonies were conducted in and around these springs. We would disrobe during these times and initially shyness was the norm. After multiple sessions participants shed their clothes with no trepidation.

So when, after many rounds of prayer with tobacco and alcohol, we were instructed to disrobe and rub a candle over our bodies we didn't hesitate. He informed us that this procedure would infuse the candles with our essence and energies. The candles were arranged around the perimeter of the altar and lit. They also warmed the space somewhat and provide a pleasant glow to the atmosphere. As they burned, the Tita would indicate a certain candle and announce that the person associated with the candle required intervention for such and such condition or would benefit from other treatments. When he indicated my candle, he said, "You want to quit your practice, but you cannot. You cannot un-be who or what you are."

I had decided prior to this event that I would quit my shamanic work and focus on film work. My intention, during this event, was to film the ceremony and not participate. But as the ceremony got underway Lily insisted that I participate. I acquiesced and was drawn into the event. I had not discussed my decision to curtail my practice with anyone, so I was taken aback by his proclamation.

The ceremony drew to its conclusion in the early morning hours. We were given short bundles of greenery and instructed to scrub our bodies with it, followed by a ceremonial mock thrashing and singeing with lit bundles of alcohol-drenched greenery. When it came my turn, Lily addressed the Tita saying, "*Quema este un poquito.*" Burn this one a little.

The Tita is on the right wearing white pants and to the left is his assistant. The candles we lit are seen at the front of the alter.

He proceeded to do just that. First, I was sprayed down with alcohol then thrashed thoroughly with the greenery to the delight of the other participants. He drenched the bundle with alcohol and lit it afire. With this burning bundle, he ran it over my bare skin, then again sprayed alcohol over me. The pain was exquisite like a bad sunburn sprayed with alcohol.

That was not the end of my ordeal. The Tita refueled the bundle with alcohol, lit it, and instructed me to extinguish the fire with my hands. I did as instructed, and when it was accomplished he turned to Lily and said, *"Ah si, este si."* (Ah, yes, this one yes.) At the time I did not comprehend the special treatment. Later I understood I was being tested. There is a perception that Shamans can handle burning coals with bare hands without being burned.

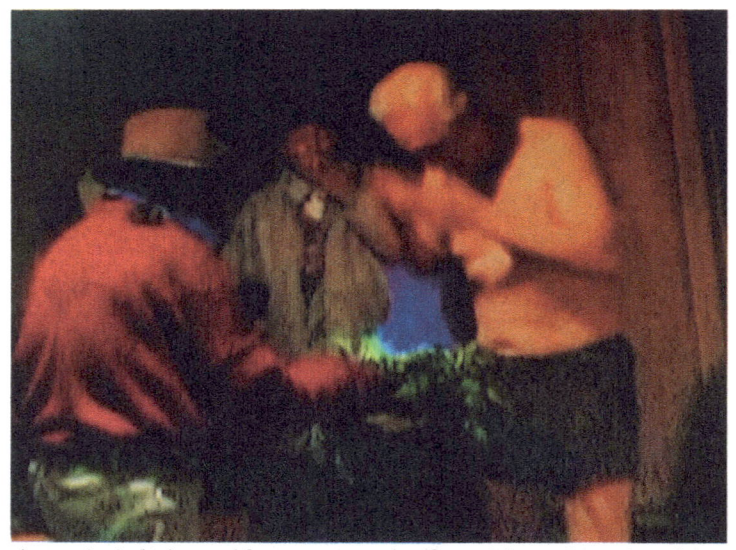

Antonio is being told to put out the fire with my bare hands.

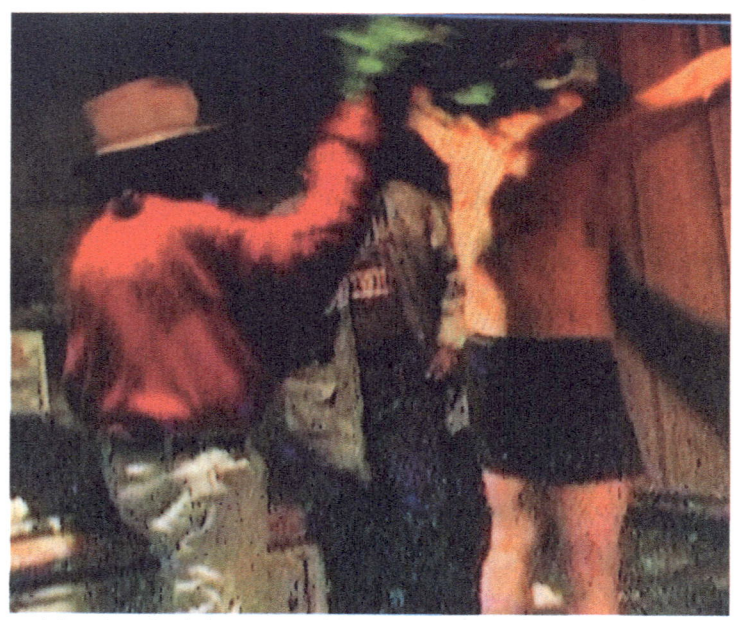

Tita thrashed Antonio with the greenery then drenched the Bundle with alcohol, lit it afire, and ran it over his bare skin.

This ceremony was about cleansing and purification. Since then, I have felt that this event provided me the most meaningful ritual I had experienced up to that time. I did feel spiritually cleansed and purified by fire and the ritual I had undergone. The act of personal sacrifice in terms of atonement is missing from our contemporary religious. After my experience, I better understood the biblical applications of sacrifice.

Chapter 29

Healing Journey

Helena performed a ritual to create a sacred space for our session to heal a problem I was having with sciatica. She used sage to smudge the room and gathered her healing tools. She chose half a dozen AVs (altered vibration healing wands). She placed a small one on my third eye beneath a headband.

Placed in my right and left hand were other AVs that felt like intense focused energy ran through them like electricity through a high voltage cable. Another AV placed on my chest completed a circuit of energy through the four AVs. I felt the energy flow along my vertical and horizontal axis.

Helena placed her fingertips on my back. I felt the energy build and the area where the problem was located pulse. Lying there, I succumbed to the soothing vibrations. Before long the pain disappeared. It was healed. And I had the realization that for me to remain truly healed I had to accept that I was heal, then in fact it was true. I did accept it as true and knew it to be so.

Then I was told, "Go," and understood that as "Go, you are healed," and was being told to go to the light that had appeared. I floated toward a source of light and entered a vortex of color.

There I joined many people. Some of the people walked against the sides of the rotating vortex. Others floated toward the light.

While moving toward the light, someone asked me, "Why are you floating?"

I answered, "Why are you walking?"

Those that walked went in endless circles within the vortex trying to stay upright and walk against the movement. Those that floated went quickly to the light.

The closer I got to the light, I felt first the movement of air over my body then a great wind pressing against me. My clothes, hair, and skin tore from my body until I was without flesh. Muscles, tendon, and organs tore from my bones, and finally, atom by atom, my physical form no longer exists. I have become all vibration. I am an energy form riding the solar winds, being swept toward the infinite. The light enfolds me and all movement ceases. I feel the oneness.

I am asked, "How do you feel?"

I pause to give this question consideration and realize I don't feel anything. I simply am. I am.

I want to remain there but am told, "No, you cannot remain here. You must return."

I asked, "Why?"

I am told, "Because you are not yet dead. It was not your time so you must return. But when you die, you will be able to remain here."

Only reluctantly do I return or attempt to return as I felt stuck between the worlds.

I don't know if my eyes were open or closed, but I could see the light fixture above me as I lay there. It was in this world and that world as both the fixture and the place within the light. Everything else around it appeared changed yet familiar. It appeared renewed as if I were seeing everything anew.

I hovered between the worlds. Helena spoke to me. At

some point she had turned on the light, and the room again became the space of light and the fixture. Again, I descended.

Earlier, while looking into the light, I had floated towards, I had to avert my eyes as I knew the light of God and that my eyes could not endure that light. And that is why people cannot see God.

Later I started to record this and found I was still not fully present. It took some time to fully emerge into ordinary reality.

Chapter 30

The Reluctant Shaman

My entry into the shamanic world was neither planned nor anticipated. And the idea of a shamanic practice remained the furthest notion of where or what I intended for my life. It unfolded unbeknownst to me as the result of a lifetime of experiences, education, interests, occupation, and temperament. Following the time of the prophetic Great Cat appearances, occurrences in my life began to be more shamanic related.

Later, visions, dreams, and events guided me into a labyrinth of twists and turns with no visible signs to a way out from this confusing path. Told during meditation to acquire a drum, even though I had never played a drum, I did and then visions directed me to play it. Also directed how to construct the mallets, I did as I was shown. Two mallets were required, and I wondered but did not ask why two mallets for a frame drum, but sometime later the reason revealed itself.

Much time followed the use of my drum, and I found I had acquired a personal connection to it. I found my drum to be a complex instrument with many voices and a powerful tool. It is as the horse that carries one into and along the shamanic journey. Shamans around the world employ the drum in their rituals and ceremonies. The drum creates the space and maintains the vibrational energy of an altered state of consciousness, enabling the Shaman and the participant to enter into it. Clarity of mind and healing energies are activated leading to spiritual growth and well-being. A large majority of mental health issues are from a spiritual wounding and so require a spiritual intervention. Many of my clients who had been treated in the traditional model for years have angrily declared, "Why didn't they do this with me?" referring to the shamanic journey.

I began my practice and very quickly had many clients as word of mouth brought clients seeking healing from past wounding. I became quite skilled in the process and gained confidence and with my tools, mainly my drum.

During a trip to Florida, I had occasion to perform a memorial ceremony for Helena's mother who had just passed. During the event, while drumming, another drummer manifested to me. He wanted to drum with me. He told me he would teach me a new way to drum, but for now he would drum along with me. He said he would take one part, and I would take the other.

It was difficult for me to let go of control. But he encouraged me to allow him freedom by relaxing and staying focused on the rhythm, and he would play his part. As I let go, the tone of the drumming changed. I watched him drum and could hear him drum his part as I drummed the rhythm. It felt out of control at times but remained consistent.

Helena had been sitting in prayerful meditation, and on completion, she informed me she had seen a drummer playing a ceremonial drum. Then a monk appeared, and she joined him in the universal dance of life. She also informed me that my drumming had changed radically from what I had been doing.

A short time later, returning to Colorado and during a journey session, the spirit drummer returned to me and told me he was my teacher. He asked if I wanted to see him, and I said yes. A dark man appeared then, a Native American man. He asked me what I would like him to look like. I said an ancient Chinese master. He appeared as a slender well-muscled man, old, wrinkled and with no hair on his face or head.

He told me the first thing I had to learn was focus and discipline to maintain a steady beat. Then I had to learn the different voices of my drum, and now he would teach me point and counterpoint, also call and response. I was also directed to the different levels of vibrational sounds, and then I heard a vibrational tone as a steady hum aside from the other two parts, the rhythm, and the harmony.

He told me the reason I was instructed (when I first started drumming) to construct and use two mallets was that one was for me and the other for my companion spirit drummer. Then we drummed.

Chapter 31

AK-47

Nearing the end of my ramblings, I have resisted this section not wanting to enter the fray we are currently experiencing. But there is ample indication that the era we are currently living in is fraught with what I will refer to as the era of unreality. We presently face the worst economic crisis since the Great Depression. The worst pandemic in a hundred years is decimating the U. S. population at 771,000 plus deaths at the time of this writing. During the last presidency, fringe groups spewed delusional and farcical claims of Satan-worshiping, of politicians running child-trafficking rings, and of the God-chosen president (Trump) being in office to root them out. And there were proclamations that Bill Gates had put chips into the COVID-19 vaccine.

Also, I am reticent to even consider this looming possibility. We are one gunshot away from a major tragic and provocative event. January 6, 2020, a mob of far-right protesters and white supremacists descended on the capitol at the invitation of Donald Trump with the intention of overturning a legitimate election, claiming that it had been stolen. That claim had been thrown out by at least sixty courts, yet the president continued to press for civil unrest. In a speech on that fateful day, he incited the mob to become terrorists and to march on the capital to fight. Which they did, and it culminated in the death of many people.

Many of these protesters came armed and with hate-filled intentions of inflicting harm on their perceived enemy, the American government. The situation escalated to a dangerous riot for all concerned. Had one of these armed insurgents, fueled by mob mentality and misplaced zeal, fired their weapons, even in the air, all hell would have broken loose. Gunfire from all quarters would have erupted, and the event would have turned even more deadly and bloody. We were one gunshot away from a civil war.

It is now acceptable, thanks to the then president's behavior, to admit and act on one's racial biases. Militia groups and individuals on the fringe are declaring their beliefs openly and without concern for consequences. The GOP is enacting bills to restrict minority voting under the guise of protecting voting integrity, despite findings that there were no voting irregularities. The nation is blatantly divided, and the danger of a civil war is not just a ridiculous notion. The proliferation of guns and lack of discretion with daily news about gun-related incidents is alarming.

There is now "truthiness," fake news, fake facts, and gross distortion of reality as we have known it. Everyone is having to decide for themselves what is truth, while their perceptions are being manipulated by outside forces with the intent to create a desired reality. Social media play a large role in determining the truth of what is being disseminated and certain political leaders create the narrative and script to be followed, ignoring facts to suit their agenda.

David Lane, a political organizer, states that America's choices are "to be faithful to Jesus or to pagan secularism." This comes with the caveat that a right-minded elite of religiously pure individuals should aim to capture the levers of government. They should then use that power to rescue society from eternal darkness and reshape it in accord with a divinely approved view of righteousness.

Senator Josh Hawley, a staunch supporter of the religious right and presidential wannabe, promotes the idea that freedom is the freedom to conform to what he and his preferred religious authorities know to be right. Sound familiar?

A medical professional working the frontlines attending to severely ill COVID-19 patients reports that these same people who cannot breathe and are being kept alive on ventilators are the ones who had stated the virus is a hoax. Even though near the end of Trump's presidency there had been 1.7 million deaths and 79 million cases worldwide as reported by the World Health Organization, his followers still believed the fiction fed to the electronic media. If one cannot discern fact from fiction at a personal level, how can one grasp more abstract issues such as climate change, state of the economy, or the pandemic? Post fake news, distorted facts, and newly stimulated primitive beliefs, our entire social environment has become spectacular fallacy and make-believe.

We are in perilous times where truthfulness is required for our existence. Today, illusion and delusion rule the day. We are at a point and time in history where the future of mankind is being determined and reshaped rapidly and more profoundly than ever before.

Chapter 32

Return Home

In what appears to be a hopeless morass is a unique opportunity for each per son to be involved in the solutions to this bleak outlook. Once again, I issue the call for Farseers to join the world community of Shamans, Healers, medicine people, spiritual leaders, and concerned warriors who are engaged in the endeavor to create a sustainable world for all. To become a Farseer requires no training, no affiliation, one simply assumes the role and educates oneself to the issues, and recruits others to become Farseers and join the world community of concerned advocates. It is important for each person to know that they are not alone in this engagement. Around the world indigenous peoples, governments, and other concerned citizens of the world are uniting to address the issues and to develop solutions. When enough people become active, the energy will shift in favor of sustainability. If nothing else, remember this, every little thing one does has an impact. Save ten gallons of water a day, don't think of how much one uses but how much one wastes. Do not recycle plastic, 90 percent ends up in the ocean or atmosphere. Demand that the producers of plastic take accountability for their product. Seemingly small gestures times a million people make a difference. Turn off lights and electronics when not in use. Become involved in whatever way you can. Xeriscaping conserves diminishing supplies of water and eliminates the need for fertilizers that run off lawns polluting the streams, rivers, and oceans, the very precious water we need. Avoid insecticides. They are all a damaging part of the ecosystem that sustains us. When the insects vanish the food chain collapses. So much of our food relies on insects. In some parts of the country, bees are trucked in to pollinate crops due to the absence of native bees.

Every aspect of the health of our planet is at risk. The vastness of the issues is complex and requires that every individual takes part in the solutions. Every individual is equally at risk.

For a more in-depth look at where we are at now in terms of the state of our planet, David Attenborough and Johan Rockstrom present a comprehensive documentary, *Breaking Boundaries: The Science of Our Planet*, directed by Jon Clay, that is both chilling and a call to action for all. It concludes that the next decade will determine the fate of our planet and our existence.

So many stories, so little time. You have joined me on a meandering journey in hopes of furthering the understanding of the Shaman from a more intimate point of view. The role of the Twenty-First Century Western Shaman must, by way of evolution, incorporate the time in which we live as well as the well-founded principles and practices of those who have preceded us. I am indebted to those who have gone before. I am forever cognizant of the past in the present and the present in a future we endeavor to shape. The deeper we delve, by whatever means, into the darkest recesses of humanity, the greater our understanding. With that we may hope for a meaningful resolution to our genetic predisposition to self-destruction. What remains for me now is the final phase of my quest, the return home. I leave you with this entry from my dream journal that seems an appropriate parting of ways.

Author's Dream of 1996

I am playing with a tiger cub that is without its mother. Someone has asked me to take care of it. I am also in my youth, and we spend a lot of time playing and enjoying ourselves. The cub is a magnificent yellow-orange color with bold black stripes and intense-looking eyes.

After some time, it is necessary that I depart to join the military and leave the tiger behind.

Time passes quickly, and I am being discharged from the military. An old friend, Sonny, is with me as we pack our duffel bags. We arrive home, get off the bus, and enter a building. After passing through a large busy room, we enter a long hall. The further we move through the hall, the darker it becomes and more natural, like a tunnel through rock.

The tunnel widens to a spacious cave. I see something moving in the darkness. It moves toward us, and we hear growling sounds. As it nears, it takes the form of a large powerful dark cat pacing in front of us and is blocking our passage. We feel fear. Sonny manages to skirt around the cat and flees further into the tunnel.

The cat draws nearer, and I see the color of a tiger emerge. It is familiar. Even though I am frightened, I reach out and extend my hand. The tiger sniffs my hand tentatively, and I then recognize it from the distinctive coloring and markings as the tiger cub fully grown.

The tiger is no longer menacing, and I scratch its head and back. The tiger rolls onto its back, and I scratch its stomach. The tiger starts to laugh in a human voice, and we again enjoy playing. I am overcome with joy to be back in the company of tiger. I am home.

Antonio conducting a memorial service in the Rocky Mountains.

Bibliography

Bailey, Paul. *Ghost Dance Messiah*. Tuscon: Westernlore "Press, 1986.

Campbell, Joseph. *The Hero with a Thousand Faces*. 2nd ed., Princeton: Princeton University Press, 1968.

Castaneda, Carlos. *The Active Side of Infinity*. New York: HarperCollins Books, 1998.

Edinger, Edward F. *Anatomy of the Psyche: Alchemical Symbolism in Psychotherapy*. La Salle: Open Court Publishing Company, 1985.

———.*Ego and Archetype: Individuation and the Religious Function of the Psyche*. Boston: Shambala Publications, Inc., 1972.

Eliade, Mircea. *Shamanism: Archaic Techniques of Ecstasy*. Translated by Willard R. Trask. Foreword by Wendy Doniger. Princeton: Princeton University Press, 1972.

Grof, Stanislav. *The Adventure of Self Discovery: Dimensions of Consciousness and New Perspectives in Psychotherapy and Inner Exploration*. Albany: State University of New York Press, 1988.

Jung, C.G. *The Archetype and the Collective Unconscious*. 2nd ed., translated by R. F. C. Hull. Princeton: Princeton University Press, 1969.

Jung, Emma, Marie-Louise von Franz. *The Grail Legend*. 2nd ed., translated by Andrea Dykes. Boston: SIGO Press, 1970.

Franz, Marie-Louise von. *Alchemy: An Introduction to the Symbolism and the Psychology*. Toronto: Inner City Books, 1980.

About Antonio

Antonio has been graced by a love of Shamanism that infuses all areas of his life. He leads individuals and groups in shamanic journeys, rites of passage, death-rebirth rituals, and drumming circles. He performs weddings and funeral ceremonies. He has been a guest lecturer on shamanism at various universities. He's guided groups from around the world to sacred places in Ecuador and the southwestern United States. Antonio has been influenced by his work with Ecuadorian and American Shamans, including the Lakota Shaman Joseph High Eagle, who gave him his medicine name.

Early in his life, Antonio trained as a medical specialist in the military and served as a Green Beret with the Special Forces. This led to a medical license as an RN, and employment as a supervisor in a forensic unit and later as an RN at a university psychiatric hospital. His intense experiences in the forensic unit inspired him to write a compelling novel *The Gatekeeper* and to found and direct a performing arts company for detained youth offenders.

Antonio's life is filled with a creative passion which he's expresses through artistic endeavors such as painting murals, composing music, filming a documentary, and sculpting. He's also been involved in many writing projects, including authoring a children's book *Death of the Last Dragon*.

It is not easy to capture in words who Antonio is. Perhaps "outside of the box" is a phrase that best describes him.

Contact Antonio:

Email: aarguello@comcast.net
Website: www.wayofthecrow.com
Facebook: www.facebook.com/thewayofthecrow

Made in the USA
Columbia, SC
31 October 2022